THE CRUSADER AND CORSAIR

Martyn Chorlton

AMBERLEY

First published 2018

Amberley Publishing
The Hill, Stroud, Gloucestershire, GL5 4EP
www.amberley-books.com

Copyright © Martyn Chorlton, 2018

The right of Martyn Chorlton to be identified as the
Author of this work has been asserted in accordance with
the Copyright, Designs and Patents Act 1988.

ISBN 978 1 4456 8107 8 (print)
ISBN 978 1 4456 8108 5 (ebook)

British Library Cataloguing in Publication Data.
A catalogue record for this book is available from the
British Library.

Origination by Amberley Publishing.
Printed in Great Britain.

Contents

Introduction   4

The Chance Vought F-8 Crusader Story   5

F-8 Crusader Technical Information   51

The Ling-Temco-Vought A-7 Corsair Story   54

A-7 Corsair Technical Information   94

Glossary   96

Introduction

This is the story of two incredible aircraft which, between them, served for nearly six decades. The Vought/LTV F-8 Crusader and its alter-ego, the LTV A-7 Corsair II, were a pair of outstanding combat aircraft. They served with the US Navy, USMC and the USAF between 1957 and 1993 and, beyond that, with the French Aéronavale and Philippine Air Force and the Portuguese and Greek Air Forces; the latter's A-7s were only retired in 2014.

In US hands, the Crusader would see action during the Cuban Missile Crisis and Vietnam, while the tough A-7 also served extensively in South East Asia, and beyond in the skies over Grenada, the Lebanon, Libya and as late as Operation Desert Storm during the first Gulf War.

The F-8 Crusader was the first US Navy aircraft capable of sustaining supersonic flight and also the first to push through 1,000 mph in level flight. The smaller, subsonic A-7 Corsair II brought continuity in US Navy hands by replacing the A-4 Skyhawk, the Douglas A-1 Skyraider and North American F-100 Super Sabre combined in USAF service, right up to 1993.

The Chance Vought F-8 Crusader Story

Vought Origins

First established by Chauncey Milton 'Chance' Vought and 'Birdseye' Lewis in 1917, the Vought Aircraft Company has been the subject of multiple buy-outs and name changes right up to the present day. Chance M. Vought was the chief engineer at the Wright Company before setting out on his own, his company quickly establishing itself by taking advantage of the sudden surge of interest in aviation after the end of the First World War. Early aviation successes included the VE-7 Bluebird trainer, one of which became the first US Navy aircraft to operate from a commissioned carrier, the USS *Langley*, on 17 October 1922. The first of a famous line of aircraft named 'Corsair' began with the O2U in 1926 and the first of several take-overs of Vought took place in 1928 when the company was bought by the United Aircraft & Transport Corporation.

Charles M. Vought passed away in 1930 but his company continued on unabated through the Great Depression. By then located in East Hartford, Connecticut, the 1934 Air Mail Act forced the United Aircraft & Transport Corporation to subdivide. The United Aircraft Corporation was formed and this included Vought. As a result, the company was moved again, this time to Stratford, Connecticut, in 1939, the home of the Sikorsky Division, and Vought-Sikorsky was created.

Chauncey Milton 'Chance' Vought, an American aviation pioneer and engineer (26 February 1890 – 25 July 1930). (*R. L. Ward Collection*)

5

Prior to this move, a new, exciting fighter aircraft was taking shape on the drawing board under the designation XF4U. This superb aircraft, with its inverted gull wings, would first take flight in 1940 as the F4U Corsair and would, incredibly, remain in production until 1952. The success of this famous fighter would re-affirm Vought as a division in its own right again from 1942. In 1949, Vought moved again, this time taking over the old North American plant at Dallas, Texas, and, with continued success, became independent again as Chance Vought Aircraft Inc. in 1954.

In 1962, the company was purchased outright by James Ling to become Ling-Temco-Vought, although Vought Aeronautics, Missiles & Space would continue its work in support of the USAF under LTV Aerospace. Multiple re-organisations began from 1972; LTV Aerospace became the Vought Corporation in 1976, only to be split again in 1983 and, from the 1990s onwards, soaked up into Northrop Grumman. Today, Vought still exists as part of the Triumph Group, operating as Triumph Aerostructures – Vought Aircraft Division.

'Birdseye' Lewis, who, along with C. M. Vought, established the Lewis & Vought Corporation in 1917. (*R. L. Ward Collection*)

One of the greatest carrier-based fighters of the Second World War, the Vought F4U Corsair remained in production from 1942 to 1953 and was not withdrawn from service until 1979! (*R. L. Ward Collection*)

A Difficult Transition

While Vought was enjoying success with the F4U Corsair, the company's early attempts to embrace jet-powered designs were not wholly successful. Vought's entry into the world of jet-powered aircraft began with the F6U-1 Pirate in response to a US Navy BuAer on 5 September 1944. The specification was for a single-seat carrier-based fighter propelled by a Westinghouse 24C turbojet. A very conventional design, the Pirate had mid-mounted straight wings, installed onto a tubby fuselage housing the turbojet, complete with air intakes blended into the leading edge of the wing. Armed with four 20 mm M3 cannon in the lower nose, the prototype XF6U-1, installed with a J34-WE-22 turbojet, first flew on 2 October 1946. The J34 only produced 3,000 lbs of thrust, resulting in a 7,320 lb aircraft which was woefully underpowered, not to mention a challenge to handle. The power issue was marginally improved when an afterburning version of the J34 was installed in the third prototype; this machine first flew on 10 November 1947. A large number of modifications followed to help improve the handling and the US Navy was so optimistic that all of the 'bugs' would be ironed out that it placed a production order for sixty-five F6U-1s.

However, following the delivery of the first F6U-1 to the US Navy for evaluation in 1949, it was quickly discovered that the Pirate fell well short of being a useful operational aircraft and, from the original production order, only thirty aircraft were actually built.

The first-generation turbojet-powered F6U Pirate was Vought's first foray into jet-powered designs. (*R. L. Ward Collection*)

A Second Bite at the Cherry

While the Pirate did not break any barriers with regard to aeronautical advancement, Vought's second attempt at producing a high-performance shipboard jet fighter was incredibly advanced. Born from a US Navy requirement for an aircraft capable of flying at 600 mph at 40,000 ft issued on 1 June 1945, Vought's design was given the designation 'V-346' and, once a contract had been issued for a trio of prototypes on 25 June 1945, the new fighter was known as the XF7U-1 and named Cutlass. Following the initial order, the US Navy requested a further fourteen pre-production F7U-1s on 29 July 1948. In the meantime, the first prototype was nearing completion and was first flown in September 1948, followed by the first pre-production machine on 1 March 1950.

With technology gleaned from captured German material at the end of the Second World War, in particular from the work of Messerschmitt's senior designer, Waldemar Voigt, the Cutlass had many novel features. Powered by twin Westinghouse J34 turbojets, which dominated the rear fuselage, the Cutlass featured a broad, low aspect ratio wing with twin-mounted fins. The pilot, situated well forward of the short fuselage, controlled the aircraft with hydraulically powered elevons for pitch and roll. The nose leg was incredibly long (a traditional characteristic of many naval aircraft) so as to increase the angle of attack during take-off. However, this same angle of attack was needed for landing and this was not a comfortable position for any carrier pilot. To reduce the approach speed, the Cutlass featured full-length leading edge slats and, to save space on the carrier, the outer wings could be folded in the vertical. On paper, the Cutlass appeared to be a great proposition for the US Navy, but unfortunately, like so many other naval aircraft of this period, it was underpowered; the prototype's Westinghouse J34s only produced 3,000 lbs of thrust dry and an unimpressive 4,250 lbs when the afterburners were lit.

The unique F7U Cutlass which, unlike the Pirate, was packed with advanced technology; however, it still lacked power, an essential factor for a carrier-based aircraft. (*R. L. Ward Collection*)

The first fourteen F7U-1s were quickly relegated to training duties and impressed no one, while, in the background, Vought worked hard to iron out the many faults of the original aircraft to produce the F7U-2. Eighty-eight were ordered by the US Navy but, thanks to problems with the engines, the order was cancelled. The F7U-3 was virtually a return to the drawing board for the Cutlass; this variant was larger, had a deeper fuselage and had more powerful J46 engines which produced 4,600 lbs of thrust dry and 6,100 lbs wet. However, the first sixteen F7U-3s had a pair of Allison J35-A-29 turbojets while Westinghouse overcame further development problems. First flown on 20 December 1951, the F7U-3 also had a revised cockpit with a better field of vision for the pilot and the undercarriage was beefed up to reduce the number of nose gear failures suffered by the earlier machines. The F7U-3M was the next variant and was modified to carry a quartet of Sparrow air-to-air missiles, while the F7U-P was a dedicated reconnaissance variant. Being rugged and highly manoeuvrable were the only redeeming features of the Cutlass, which was furnished with many unfaltering nicknames before the type began a rapid withdrawal from the US Navy, beginning in 1956.

Vought had made very few friends in the US Navy with the Pirate and the Cutlass and the odds of the company overcoming this poor reputation were slim; however, work had already begun on a replacement which would soon put the memory of these early generation jet fighters to bed.

The V-383

It was while Vought were still struggling to improve the Cutlass in September 1952 that the US Navy issued a request for another new fighter capable of reaching Mach 0.9 at sea level, Mach 1.2 at 30,000 ft, a climb rate of 25,000 ft per minute and a landing speed of 100 kts (115 mph). This proposal was issued to a number of US aircraft manufacturers, although only Grumman, McDonnell and Vought had been involved with the production of carrier-based aircraft. Under the leadership of John Russell Clark, a number of the Vought design team were put to work on the new fighter and, in total, the US Navy was bombarded with twenty-one design proposals from Convair, Douglas, Grumman, Lockheed, McDonnell, North American, Republic and Vought. The US Navy picked out four designs; these were the Grumman XF11F-2, the McDonnell F3H-G, the North American 'Super Fury' and Vought's

The mock-up XF8U-1, awaiting inspection at Dallas, Texas, in September 1953. (*R. L. Ward Collection*)

9

own design, which at the time was simply designated the V-383. In May 1953, it was announced that Vought's V-383 had won the hotly contested competition and the US Navy ordered a number of mock-ups and several wind tunnel models before looking at prototype and production contracts. On top of that, the US Navy ordered three prototypes on 29 June 1953 with the serials 138899–138901. By this stage, V-383 had been dispensed with and the designation XF8U-1 was allocated; simultaneously, a reconnaissance variant, originally known as the V-392, was ordered, which would later become the F8U-1P.

Progress was swift and a mock-up was ready for inspection at the Chance Vought Division (United Aircraft Corporation) facility at Dallas, Texas, between 16 and 18 September 1953.

The Nuts and Bolts of the V-383

Powered by a single Pratt & Whitney J57-P-11 turbojet, this powerplant was streaks ahead of the earlier Westinghouse units thanks to a dry thrust of 9,700 lb and 14,800 lb when the afterburner was engaged. However, the most novel feature of the aircraft, which we will refer to as the F-8 Crusader from now on, was its wing configuration, which was swept and high-mounted but, uniquely, could be raised to increase the angle of attack during take-off and landing. The wing could be raised to a maximum of 7 degrees and this removed the traditional nose-up attitude which made take-off and landings so challenging for naval aviators. From an aerodynamic point of view, the fuselage was actually lowered to a near horizontal position rather than the wing being raised. The variable-incidence wing was controlled by a positioning and locking handle in the cockpit, which operated a hydraulic actuator (with a pneumatic back-up), causing the wing to pivot via a hinge along the rear main spar. When raised, the faired forward centre section of the wing stuck out into the airstream, meaning that it both worked as a speed brake and maintained a high angle of attack. Simultaneously, when the wing was raised, both the ailerons and all leading edge surfaces were lowered to an angle of 25 degrees and the small flaps inboard of the ailerons (hydraulically powered 'flaperons') also lowered to approximately 30 degrees, which increased the lift of the wing by some margin. After take-off, as the wing was retracted, all flying surfaces were returned to their normal positions and traditional roles. The prototype, now designated the XF8U-1 (later XF-8A), had a 42 degree swept wing, which was 350 sq/ft in size and had an anhedral of 5 degrees. There were no control surfaces on the outer wing panels, as these could be hydraulically folded to the vertical to save space both on and below deck.

The main metal used to construct the F-8 Crusader was aluminium alloy, although 25 per cent of the fuselage and the skin of the wings were made from magnesium alloy, not to mention the extensive use of titanium. The latter was used for the core structure of the fuselage and the rear fuselage, specifically around the afterburner. An 'Area-Ruled' design, the fuselage was narrower below the wing and, as such, helped to give the F-8 good transonic performance as well as a pleasant-looking appearance.

No section of the aircraft's fuselage was unused, beginning with a comprehensive avionics bay in the nose. The cockpit sat behind and to the rear was the armament bay; both sat above the nose gear compartment. The pilot was provided with a lightweight Vought ejection seat, with access gained via a rear-hinged clamshell canopy and a set of extendable steps which were installed in the lower fuselage.

The rearward retracting nose gear, as implied earlier, was much smaller than previous naval aircraft and, like the short, strong main undercarriage, was much lighter than previous designs. The main undercarriage retracted forward and all three units had single wheels.

The centre section of the fuselage, behind the armament bay, housed fuel tanks that were slotted in either side of the engine intake, which had its main aperture directly at the lower front of the aircraft. The aircraft's remaining fuel tanks were located inside the inner sections of the wings. Beyond was the J57 turbojet, which could be conveniently accessed through the removal of the rear fuselage. The F-8 Crusader's fin was large, while the tailplane was a single-section 'all-moving' design which pivoted at a single point.

The aircraft also featured a single rear 'stinger'-type arrestor hook which could be fully retracted, a dive brake located in the lower fuselage, a retractable refuelling probe (production aircraft) in the port upper forward fuselage (concealed by a prominent bulge/fairing) and a Ram Air Turbine (RAT). The Marquardt-built RAT was located on the lower starboard side of the forward fuselage, behind the armament bay, and could be extended in flight to provide emergency electrical and hydraulic power should the need arise, and it often did, many pilots bringing battle-damaged aircraft safely home as a result.

The main internal armament of the F-8 Crusader was a quartet of Colt-Browning 20 mm Mk 12 cannon, with enough room for 144 rounds per gun. In the extreme nose was housed an AN/APG-30 radar which assisted with aiming the cannon. Directly behind the guns, on each side of the forward fuselage, was a single pylon, each of which was able to carry an AIM-9 Sidewinder, although later variants could carry a pair on an extended pylon. There was also the novel provision for a retractable rocket pack in the belly of the aircraft which was large enough to hold thirty-two 2.75 in. (70 mm) 'Might Mouse' folding-fin rockets. Intended to be used for ground attack work, or even for taking on enemy bombers, this was a feature so novel that it was barely used and the vast majority of production aircraft had the rocket pack welded shut.

The mock-up again, which presents us with a good view of the wing in the take-off and landing position and retracted for normal flight. Also note the forward extended airbrake in the upper image, which was replaced by a single air brake in the lower fuselage. (*R. L. Ward Collection*)

Above: Another view of the main wing in the raised position; note the folded outer wing panels, which were essential for saving space on board an aircraft carrier. A short, stocky undercarriage was another positive feature of the F-8 Crusader. (*R. L. Ward Collection*)

Below: An impressive array of weaponry, which included four 20 mm Colt-Browning Mk 12 cannon, four AIM-9A Sidewinders, provision for a pair of 300-gallon drop tanks and/or the capability to carry 5,000 lbs of bombs or rockets. (*R. L. Ward Collection*)

This cockpit view of an F-8E is centred by a lightweight Vought ejection seat. Access was gained via a rear-hinged clamshell canopy and a set of extendable steps which were installed in the lower fuselage. (*Joseph T. Thompson via R. L. Ward Collection*)

Maiden Flights and Into Production

The first prototype XF8U-1 (later redesignated the YF8U-1), No. 138899, made its roll-out debut in February 1955 and, after being delivered to Edwards AFB in a Douglas C-124 Globemaster, carried out its maiden flight in the capable hands of Vought's Chief Test Pilot, John W. Konrad, on 25 March. The arrival of the XF8U-1 instantly dispelled any myths as to whether Vought was up to the job of producing an effective fighter for the US Navy. On its maiden 52-minute flight, Konrad took No. 138899 through Mach 1; this was the first time an aircraft designed to be operated from a carrier had broken the speed of sound. The second prototype XF8U-1, No. 138900, which differed very little from the first aircraft, carried out its first flight on 30 September 1955, by which time this impressive machine had been christened the 'Crusader'. The third and final prototype, No. 138901, was cancelled by the US Navy but Vought built it anyway and this went on to serve as a static test airframe.

No. 138899 did the lion's share of the initial flight testing and, by the time it was retired in 1960, the aircraft had completed 508 flights. That same year, No. 138899 was donated to the Smithsonian Museum and, today, is preserved at the Seattle Museum of Flight. The second aircraft, No. 138900, managed 460 test flights before it was scrapped and it is most likely that the third, static prototype would have suffered a similar fate.

Flight testing progressed so well that the US Navy proceeded with a production order, the initial variant being designated the F8U-1 (later the F-8A, from 18 September 1962) Crusader. There were very few differences between the prototypes and these early production aircraft; the first of them, No. 140444, took to the air on the same day as the second prototype! The first dozen F-8U-1s were powered by a J57-P-12A engine but this was soon replaced by the J57-P-4A, which could belt out 16,200 lbs when the afterburner was lit.

Wasting very little time, carrier qualification testing began on board USS *Forrestal* (CVA-59) in April 1956. The fourth production aircraft, F8U-1 No. 140446, was used for the task with test pilot Commander R. W. 'Duke' Windsor in the cockpit. It was this aircraft which carried out the very first catapult launch of an F-8 Crusader on 4 April 1956. There was no doubting the Crusader's incredible performance and, before the aircraft had even entered service, the US Navy was keen to show off its potential. The World Air Speed Record was there for the taking and at that time was in American hands thanks to a North American F-100C Super Sabre which had raised the bar to 822.1 mph. However, the British Fairey FD2 research aircraft had smashed the record by over 300 mph, raising it to 1,132 mph. Undeterred, but conscious of the fact that they did not really want to give away the true performance capability of the Crusader, the US Navy focussed on the national speed record instead. Once again with 'Duke' Windsor at the controls, F8U-1 No. 141345 carried out a pair of runs over a 15-km-long course at an altitude of 40,000 ft over China Lake, California. The average speed was 1,015.428 mph: a new national record, with the bonus of the Thompson Trophy being awarded to Vought and the US Navy.

The prototype XF8U-1, No. 138899, in company with an F7U Cutlass. (*R. L. Ward Collection*)

Above: Test pilot John Konrad tucks away the undercarriage of XF8U-1 No. 138899 before embarking on another test flight. (*Chance Vought CVPR-682 via R L Ward Collection*)

Below: The second prototype XF8U-1, No. 138900, under tow prior to carrying out its maiden flight on 30 September 1955. (*Chance Vought CVPR-542 via R. L. Ward Collection*)

Above: Titled 'Five fingers for 500 Flights...' this is John Konrad after completing his 500th flight at the controls of an F-8 Crusader. (*Chance Vought CVPR-2261 via R. L. Ward Collection*)

Below: A rare image of the first production F8U-1 Crusader, No. 140444, which first flew on 30 September 1955. Its flying career was short; the aircraft was written off at Edwards AFB on 1 February 1956. (*Chance Vought via R. L. Ward Collection*)

Crusader Into Service

The first F8U-1s entered service with the US Navy's VX-3 (Air Development Squadron 3), based at NAS Oceana, Virginia, on 28 December 1956. At least eleven F8U-1s served with VX-3, a number of them conducting further carrier qualification work on the USS *Franklin D. Roosevelt* in April 1957. A few weeks earlier, the first F8U-1 Crusaders began to arrive at operational squadrons; the first of them was VF-32 at NAS Cecil Field, Florida, closely followed by VF-154 (initially named the 'Grandslammers' in honour of the F-8 and then later renamed the 'Black Knights'), VF(AW)-3 and VF-211 respectively. VF-32 had the honour of being the first squadron to operate the F-8 on board a carrier when they carried out a Mediterranean tour on the USS *Saratoga* in late 1957.

In the meantime, VX-3 was putting the F-8 through its paces and, unfortunately, out of the eleven aircraft assigned to the unit, four would be lost in accidents. The first of them, No. 141350, was ditched into the Atlantic only three days after joining VX-3 on 30 January 1957. On a more positive note, a pair of VX-3 F8U-1s, with Captain Robert G. Dose and Lt Cdr Paul Miller at the controls, carried out an impressive couple of sorties on 6 June 1957. Taking off from USS *Bon Homme Richard* (CVA-31) off the Californian coast, the two Crusaders flew due east to the USS *Saratoga* off the Florida coast in a record time of 3 hours 28 minutes, which included air-to-air refuelling over Texas en route. The two airmen were met on the USS *Saratoga* by US President Dwight D. Eisenhower.

The first F-8s to join the USMC did so in December 1957 when VMF-122 'Crusaders', stationed at MCAS Beaufort, received the type in place of the FJ Fury. VMF-312, VMF-333 and VMF-334 were also re-equipped with the F8U-1 Crusader not long after.

An F8U-1 Crusader of VX-3 leaves the starboard catapult of the USS *Franklin D. Roosevelt.* (*Chance Vought (CVPR-1227) via R. L. Ward Collection*)

Above: The first operational squadron to fly the F8U-1 Crusader was VF-32 out of Cecil Field, Florida. This aircraft, No. 142413 '214/K', crashed on 17 October 1957. (*Chance Vought (CVPR-1433) via R. L. Ward Collection*)

Below: A pair of F8U-1 Crusaders of VF-124, operating out of NAS Moffett Field, California, fly a tight formation over San Francisco. (*Official US Navy photograph via R. L. Ward Collection*)

Recce Bird

Before the F8U-1 variant had found its feet, it was quickly recognised that the Crusader would be well suited to the photographic reconnaissance role. This new variant would be designated the F8U-1P (later RF-8A) and would be completely unarmed, relying on its speed to get it out of trouble, in keeping with the tradition established by specialised reconnaissance aircraft of the past. To accommodate a bank of aerial cameras, the lower forward fuselage was made broader and was flattened off, making room for a trio of CAX-12 Trimetrogen (KA-66) and a pair of K-17 vertical cameras. As the aircraft and its role evolved, other camera fits were installed but the most common in service was one vertical (KA-51, -53 or -62), one starboard or port-facing oblique and a forward-facing oblique (KA-45 or 51). As the area-ruled profile of the F8U-1P was disrupted by the fuselage redesign, a hump/fairing was installed directly above the leading edge of the wing to compensate.

The prototype YF8U-1P was No. 141363, the thirty-second production F8U-1, an aircraft that went on to achieve a busy service career and today has been preserved at the Pima Air and Space Museum, Tucson, Arizona. The first production F8U-1Ps (RF-8A from September 1962) were delivered to VFP-61 in September 1957, and before the year was out, the unit began a tour on board USS *Midway*. Prior to this, another record-breaking attempt was planned: this time the US coast-to-coast, which would be flown from California to New York. Two aircraft would carry out the task: F8U-1P No. 144608 with Major John H. Glenn

VFP-61 show off a batch of new F8U-1P (later RF-8A) Crusaders in late 1957. None of this group survived their service. The nearest two aircraft were both lost in action; No. 144623 '925/PP' was shot down over North Vietnam in 1967 and No. 164616 '922/PP' was brought down over Laos in 1968. (*Chance Vought via R. L. Ward Collection*)

The pilot of a VFP-63 RF-8A Crusader checks his camera switches before embarking on another recce sortie from the USS *Coral Sea*. (*Official US Navy photograph (Light Photoron Sixty-Three) via R. L. Ward Collection*)

F8U-1P Crusader No. 144608 as flown by Major John H. Glenn USMC during Project Bullet. (*Chance Vought via R. L. Ward Collection*)

Above: Lt Charles Demmler takes on fuel from an AJ-2 Savage tanker of VAH-11 during a US coast-to-coast flight on 16 July 1957 with Major John H. Glenn's aircraft tucked in close behind. (*Chance Vought via R. L. Ward Collection*)

Below: A nice study of a pair of RF-8A Crusaders of VFP-63, captured on 20 October 1965 during Detachment B aboard USS *Ticonderoga*. (*Official US Navy photograph (46513) via R. L. Ward Collection*)

RF-8A Crusader No. 144616 '934/PP' of VFP-3 launching from USS *Constellation*. (*Official US Navy photograph via R. L. Ward Collection*)

USMC at the controls, accompanied by Lt Charles Demmler US Navy in a F8U-1. The record flight was named 'Project Bullet' as this was also a test of the full-power endurance of the Crusader and the potential average speed would be faster than the muzzle velocity of a .45 calibre bullet! As the flight was not about economy, the Crusaders would have to refuel three times en route and a trio of AJ-2 Savage tankers provided the support. The flight was carried out on 16 July 1957, with both aircraft taking off from Los Angeles. All was going well until Demmler broke the refuelling probe of his Crusader over Albuquerque, New Mexico, giving himself no option other than to land prematurely. Glenn pressed on and, after a flight of just 3 hours 23 minutes 8.4 seconds, landed at Floyd Bennett Field, New York, having achieved an impressive average speed of 725.25 mph. For this flight, Glenn, who among other things, would go on to become the first American in space, was awarded the Distinguished Flying Cross.

The 'Fleet' Crusader Evolves

The F8U-1E was the next production variant; it was subsequently redesignated the F-8B. The 'E' suffix was short for 'Electronic Equipment', which basically entailed the installation of an AN/APS-67 radar. This radar gave the F8U-1E a restricted all-weather capability, and was housed behind a new all-plastic nose cone. The first F8U-1E made its maiden flight on 3 September 1958 and this mark retained the F8U-1's J-57-P-4A engine and the armament fit.

The next variant, the F8U-2 (later F-8C), raised the bar with regard to the Crusader's evolution into one of the US Navy's best fleet fighter aircraft. Making its maiden flight as the YF8U-2 on 20 August 1957, the Crusader had more power thanks to the J57-P-16, which was rated at 10,700 lbs dry and 16,900 lbs when the afterburner was lit. This amount of power demanded some modifications, beginning with a pair of air scoops installed above the afterburner section of the engine, either side of the rudder, which provided extra cooling. A pair of ventral strakes was also installed below the rear fuselage in an effort to improve directional stability, although many service pilots reported that they made no difference to the Crusader's handling. Armament-wise, a modified missile rack was installed either side of the forward fuselage which was capable of carrying up to four Sidewinders rather than the standard two. However, this was also a modification that did little to improve the aircraft; most service pilots only carried a pair of Sidewinders in combat, because four proved not to be worth the extra weight and the resulting fuel consumed. Performance figures for the F8U-2 were impressive, thanks to the J-57-P-16 engine. The aircraft had a maximum speed of 1,105 mph (Mach 1.67) at 35,000 ft and a combat ceiling of 52,000 ft.

However, the F8U-2 was not the fastest version of the Crusader; that honour fell to the F8U-2N (later F-8D), thanks to an even more powerful J57-P-20 which had the same dry thrust as the J-57-P4A but an uprated reheat of 18,000 lbs. This gave the F8U-2N a maximum speed of 1,228 mph (Mach 1.86) at 35,000 ft and an increased combat ceiling of 53,400 ft. The 'N' suffix stood for 'Night' as this was the intended role for this new mark, which was

Originally designated as the F8U-1E before becoming the F-8B Crusader, this variant differed from the F-8A in having an AN/APS-67 radar. This is F-8B No. 145486 in service with VMF-235 of the USMC at Beaufort, South Carolina. (*R. L. Ward Collection*)

Above: The first production F8U-2 (F-8C), No. 145546, lands at Dallas. (*Chance Vought via R. L. Ward Collection*)

Below: Production F8U-2 (F-8C) Crusader No. 145573, which entered service with VF-84 at Oceana, Virginia. Another Crusader destined to have a short flying career, this aircraft crashed on 17 November 1959. (*Chance Vought via R. L. Ward Collection*)

After serving with the NATC at NAS Patuxent River, F-8C No. 145546 was despatched to NASA and re-registered as N802NA. (*R. L. Ward Collection*)

A four-ship of F-8D Crusaders of VF-82 over the Mediterranean, during a cruise aboard the carrier USS *Shangri-La*. (*Official US Navy photograph (PR.8588) via R. L. Ward Collection*)

A splash of colour from the rear fuselage of F-8D Crusader No. 148656 '2/WD' of VMF(AW)-212, USMC. (*R. L. Ward Collection*)

An F-8D Crusader, in service with NATC, turning finals at Patuxent River in 1966. (*Official US Navy Photograph (Wise PHC (1119076)) via R. L. Ward Collection*)

furnished with an upgraded Motorola APQ-63 radar, a new fire control system and a new push-button autopilot. One new external feature was the introduction of the AN/AAS-15 IRST (Infrared Search and Track) sensor, which was mounted directly above the radome in front of the cockpit. Another significant feature of the F8U-2N was the APC (Approach Power Compensator), which was designed to make deck landings much easier for the pilot, especially those who were less experienced. The APC had the ability to keep the aircraft at a fixed airspeed (within a 4 knot bracket) when approaching the carrier. The system could only be engaged when the main wing was in the up position and involved the combined use of an accelerometer, a computer, a servo amplifier and an actuator, all of which were controlled through a panel in the cockpit. Working in conjunction with the Crusader's inbuilt angle of attack detector, the APC detected any variation that would affect the approach speed and adjust the power accordingly. Armament was the same as the F8U-2, although with the F8U-2N the capability to carry the ventral rocket pack was completely deleted and it was replaced by a fuel tank that raised the aircraft's capacity to 1,348 gallons. The first F8U-2N took to the air on 16 February 1960 and a total of 152 were built between June 1960 and January 1962.

F8U-2NE (F-8E) Crusader No. 149147 of VF-51 over the US aircraft carrier USS *Constellation*. The aircraft was forced to ditch off the USS *Hancock* in the Gulf of Tonkin on 25 March 1967. (*Official US Navy Photograph via R. L. Ward Collection*)

Some subtle external differences are revealed in this view of an F8U-2N in the foreground and an F8U-2NE to the rear. (*Official US Navy photograph via R. L. Ward Collection*)

The final production variant of the Crusader was the capable F8U-2NE (late F-8E), the first example of which flew on 30 June 1961. The prototype YF8U-2NE was converted from F8U-1 No. 143710. Classed as a multi-role fighter-bomber, the F8U-2NE had a larger and more powerful APQ-94 search and fire-control radar housed in an enlarged radome; the latter increased the length of the aircraft by 3 inches. A small hump, located on the top of the main wing for the F8U-1P, was used to house avionics for the AGM-12 Bullpup air-to-surface missile, although this was very rarely used in combat. To increase the Crusader's air-to-ground capability, a pair of underwing pylons were installed, each of them strong enough to carry a 2,000 lb bomb. The F8U-2NE was cleared up to a weight of 5,000 lbs and this usually entailed four 1,000 lb bombs and eight 5 in. Zuni FFAR unguided rockets, which were carried on the forward missile pylons. 286 F-8Es were built, the last of them in the summer of 1964.

T-Bird

It seems rather odd that the option of a two-seat trainer variant of the Crusader was not on the table from the outset. By the time that the subject was looked at in closer detail, the bulk of the 1,200 Crusaders produced had been delivered to the US Navy and USMC. In 1962, the prototype F8U-2NE, No. 143710, was selected for conversion into a two-seat trainer and was initially redesignated the XF8U-1T (aka V-408). Powered by a de-rated J57-P-20 engine, which gave it the same potential performance as a standard F8U-1, the main modification work, as you would expect, was around the forward fuselage. In order to create a tandem cockpit configuration, the original pilot's position was retained with a second new cockpit positioned behind. For the pilot occupying the rear seat to maintain a good forward view, his seat was 15 inches higher than the front seat and, as a result, the aircraft had a hump-backed appearance which was contoured into an upper fairing above the main wing. To make room for the second cockpit, all of the equipment was re-positioned in the fuselage, including the ammunition tanks, although the 20 mm cannon were reduced to a

The sole example of a two-seat Crusader was originally built as an F8U-1 (F-8A), then became the prototype YF8U-2NE before becoming the XF8U-1T (later TF-8A). Serialled 143710, the aircraft enjoyed a busy career before being lost on 28 July 1978. (*Chance Vought/ LTV via R. L. Ward Collection*)

Above: The TF-8A landing on the USS *Independence*, one of twenty-eight arrestments and touch-and-go landings made by the aircraft, all under the control of the pilot in the rear cockpit. (*Official US Navy photograph (PR-4098) via R. L. Ward Collection*)

Below: The TF-8A, No. 143710 '710/FT', (designated briefly as a YTF-8A) during its service with the NATC. (*Official US Navy photograph via R. L. Ward Collection*)

The TF-8A Crusader, No. 143710, during its tenure with NASA in the mid to late 1970s. (*NASA image via R. L. Ward Collection*)

pair, the upper cannon being removed. Both cockpits were fully furnished with a complete set of flight controls and a wind-blast shield was placed between them in the event of an emergency ejection from the front. Other modifications included a parabrake in the tail cone and low-pressure tyres which allowed for soft-field operations.

The XF8U-1T made its maiden flight on 6 February 1962 and, after briefly being redesignated the F8U-1T, was known as the TF-8A from September 1962 onwards. Despite being built under a US Navy contract, no orders were forthcoming and this was aggravated by a substantial cut in funding in 1964. Undeterred, Vought took the TF-8A on a European tour and, for a while, looked like they had secured an order in the United Kingdom for a Rolls-Royce Spey-powered version. However, the British chose the Phantom instead.

The TF-8A served as a flight test aircraft for LTV instead and was later passed on to the US Navy's NATC at Patuxent River, Maryland, before being handed over to NASA. In 1977, the TF-8A was returned to LTV to serve as a transitional trainer for the Philippine Air Force. Sadly, this unique and purposeful aircraft was lost in a training accident on 28 July 1978.

Remanufacturing – G to L

By the mid-1960s the Vietnam War was taking its toll on US Navy aircraft but the F-8 Crusader still maintained its position as a primary fighter and reconnaissance aircraft, in company with the F-4 Phantom. The latter needed a large carrier to operate from while the F-8 Crusader was able to serve on the US Navy's smaller 27C-Class aircraft carriers. As such, the US Navy kept these carriers in service longer than planned, specifically for the F-8 Crusader, and in order to keep the aircraft in the front line, an extensive remanufacturing programme was implemented. As a result, LTV was awarded a lucrative contract to refurbish and modernise all F-8 Crusaders currently in service and these would re-enter service with suffixes ranging from 'G' to 'L', although 'I' was not used.

The first batch to be remanufactured were seventy-three RF-8As, the first of which re-entered service as the RF-8G in October 1965. The only major difference, externally at least, was the addition of the ventral strakes and, internally, the J57-P-22 engine. The RF-8G would remain in service much longer than expected and was again upgraded in early 1977. A more powerful J57-P-429 engine was installed (given away by the same air scoops installed on the F-8C onwards), along with improved electrical wiring throughout, new ECM equipment and a RWR fitted to the fin.

The next batch to be remanufactured were eighty-nine F-8Ds, the first of them in 1967, which were destined to re-enter service as the F-8H later in the year. Re-engined with the J57-P-20A, the F-8H also featured the same underwing pylons as the F-8E, complete with the Bullpup fire-control system inside the hump above the main wing. The F-8H served with several Naval Air Reserve squadrons and the composite VC-13 before bowing out to the A-4L Skyhawk in 1974.

136 F-8Es were next on the agenda, remanufactured as the F-8J. Again, the J57-P-20A engine was installed, as was provision for a pair of 300-US gallon drop tanks on the underwing pylons. Another significant feature was a redesigned main wing with a much greater variable camber that had bigger hinged droops along the leading and trailing edge of the wing. The original wing's leading edge drooped by 27 degrees while this new wing drooped by an impressive 55 degrees! The large flaps and drooping ailerons were also modified to lower further (almost double their original distance), to such a degree that blown BLC (Boundary-Layer Control) was created using engine bleed air to prevent the airflow from breaking away. This same wing was installed on the Aéronavale F-8E(FN) covered later. The F-8J would be prevalent during the final eighteen months of the Vietnam War but was not destined to improve on the Crusader's MiG kill rate.

Major John Glenn's record-breaking RF-8A was one of seventy-three such aircraft which were converted into RF-8Gs. This is No. 144608, mid-conversion. (*Chance Vought/LTV via R. L. Ward Collection*)

Above: RF-8G Crusaders of VFP-63 based at NAS Miramar, California. (*Official US Navy photograph via R. L. Ward Collection*)

Below: One of eighty-nine F-8Ds converted to F-8H standard, No. 147060 initially served with VF-201 out of NAS Dallas. The aircraft was a survivor, later joining the Philippine Air Force in early 1978. (*R. L. Ward Collection*)

Five F-8J Crusaders of VF-211, operating from USS *Bon Homme Richard*, fly a tight formation for the camera. (*Official US Navy photograph via R. L. Ward Collection*)

The majority of the eighty-seven F-8K conversions served with the USMC, including this machine, No. 146990 '00/ MK' of VMF-511. (*R. L. Ward Collection*)

Like the 'new' F-8J before it, the next batch of eighty-seven F-8Cs were upgraded to the same standard as the F-8H but were actually redesignated the F-8K. The F-8K also featured new underwing pylons and a new cockpit light system. The bulk of them served with the USMC. The final part of the Crusader upgrade programme involved sixty-one F-8Bs remanufactured to F-8L standard, which involved the same modifications as the F-8K. Once again, the majority served with the USMC, although a few also found themselves in US Navy hands. There were also plans to create the F-8M, which would have been remanufactured F-8As with low flying hours; however, very few were left in service, which meant that the upgrade was pointless.

Drones

At least fifty F-8 Crusaders were converted into drones during the aircraft's service career, although very little is known about exactly what the conversion entailed. The first examples were twenty-three ex-F-8As, redesignated the DF-8A. It is known that they were fitted with the APS-67 radar and were employed as RPV target/drone directors, a number working with the Chance Vought RQM/MQM/GQM-15A Regulus II drones. Another RPV drone director conversion was to QF-8A standard; again, information is lacking as to what this entailed. Another example was the F-8A conversion to DF-8F standard, of which twenty-seven examples are known to have existed, and six F-8Ls also became drones, being redesignated the DF-8L. Operators included the US Navy's VC-7 and VC-8 and at least two were used by the Naval Missile Test Centre at Point Mugu, California.

Five F-8L Crusaders were converted to DF-8L drones, including No. 145528, which began its service career as an F8U-1E (F-8B). (*R. L. Ward Collection*)

Crusader in USN/USMC Service

VF-154 was the first Crusader-equipped unit to perform a carrier deployment in the Pacific, on USS *Hancock* in early 1958, followed by the first Atlantic deployment on USS *Saratoga*, courtesy of VF-32. July of that year saw VF-32 carry out the first operational deployment in support of a USMC landing in the Lebanon. Flying patrols over the Eastern Mediterranean, VF-32 was relieved by VMF-333 from USS *Saratoga* in September.

The F8U-1P (RF-8A) carried out its first US Navy deployment aboard USS *Midway* in late 1957 and it was this variant that would play an important role in the forthcoming Cuban Missile Crisis in October 1962. The task of flying low-level, high-speed reconnaissance missions over Cuba was carried out by aircraft from the US Navy's VFP-62 and the USMC's VMCJ-2, both operating out of NAS Cecil Field, Florida. While the high-flying Lockheed U-2 provided the initial evidence that something was afoot, it was down to the RF-8As to provide the detail and this could be only achieved down on the deck. Codenamed Blue Moon, two flights were carried out per day, the first on 23 October 1962, taking off from NAS Key West and landing at NAS Jacksonville, where the films were processed and then delivered direct to the Pentagon a few hours later. Following an unnerving stand-off, the Soviet Union agreed to remove their IRBMs, and this 'withdrawal' was also covered by the RF-8As until the 'crisis' was completely over in April 1963.

Even before the infamous Gulf of Tonkin incident early in August 1964, which effectively resulted in full-blown hostilities in Vietnam, the RF-8As of VFP-62 were carrying out low-level reconnaissance operations over Laos. A pair of RF-8As from USS *Kitty Hawk* were engaged by anti-aircraft fire. The aircraft of Lieutenant Charles F. Klusmann was hit but still managed to land safely. Lt Klusmann was in the thick of it again on 6 June, but this time the ground fire was so intense and accurate that he was forced to eject. As such, his aircraft, No. 146823, became the first Crusader to be lost to enemy action after crashing near Khang Khay Nong Pet. Captured by the Pathet Lao, Klusmann managed to escape after over eighty days in captivity and reached friendly forces on 31 August.

7 June also saw another reconnaissance operation involving a pair of RF-8As escorted by a pair of VF-111 F-8Ds from USS *Kitty Hawk*. The formation was also fired on and, in response, the F-8Ds returned fire with cannon and rockets, effectively firing the first of many rounds of the long Vietnam War. A second operation, on 7 June, involving a single RF-8A escorted by three F-8s, resulted in one of the fighters, flown by Commander Foyle W. Linn, being hit by flak and crashing. Linn was recovered by helicopter the following day.

The Gulf of Tonkin incident on 2 August 1964 is well-known for involving the US Navy destroyer USS *Maddox*, which was attacked by at least three North Vietnamese PT boats after the ship strayed close to or into North Vietnamese waters. In support of the *Maddox*, the USS *Ticonderoga* despatched four F-8Es from VF-51 and VF-53 in response. The Crusaders engaged the PT boats with cannon and rockets, sinking one of them but not before return fire hit one of the Crusaders, forcing it to land at Da Nang. Two days later, a second attack by North Vietnamese PT boats was supposed to have taken place, but there is much doubt today as to whether it actually did. Swept along by the US Government and fuelled by the press, war was inevitable. Within days, the situation escalated further when aircraft from the USS *Constellation* and *Ticonderoga* attacked the North Vietnamese PT boat bases, a strike which involved F-8 fighters and RF-8As.

As the tension and forces began to build up, Crusaders found themselves serving on every single US Navy carrier in the region in the reconnaissance role while the fighter variants also operated from the USS *Midway, Coral Sea* and *Franklin D. Roosevelt*. By early 1965, in response to increasing attacks by the Viet Cong, Operation Rolling Thunder was initiated, which involved relentless bombing missions. However, the Crusader was primarily employed in the reconnaissance role, with fighter variants providing escort and ground target suppression when needed. In the latter role, the F-8 fighter, in company with A-4 Skyhawks, was employed to attack the increasing number of North Vietnamese anti-aircraft defences. The technique was for the A-4s to launch AGM-45 Shrike missiles, which the F-8s would follow direct to the target. When the Shrike impacted, the F-8s would finish the anti-aircraft position off with cannon and Zuni rockets. It was a technique that worked well until the North Vietnamese realised that they only had to turn their radar sets off to out-fox the Shrike! North Vietnamese ground fire, which included everything from small arms fire to SAM missiles, would claim a total of forty-two US Navy F-8s and twenty RF-8s from VFP-63 plus a dozen USMC machines of VMCJ-1. All of the VFP-63 and VMCJ-1 aircraft were brought down by SAMs or flak while only three of the fighter variants were shot down by MiGs.

It was in April 1965 that the Crusader first encountered a North Vietnamese MiG in air-to-air combat. One F-8 was damaged during the mêlée and, unfortunately, a pair of F-105 Thunderchiefs fell to the MiGs. The very first confirmed US Navy kills of the Vietnam War, a pair of MiG-17s, were credited to a pair of F-4B Phantoms of VF-21 on 17 July 1965 and it would be a while before the Crusader added to the tally. The duck was eventually removed on 12 June 1966 when Commander Harold L. Mar of VF-211 brought down a MiG-17 while providing escort for an A-4 strike. A Second World War and Korean War veteran, forty-two-year-old Commander Richard 'Limpy Dick' Bellinger, the commanding officer of VF-162, brought an example of the more advanced MiG-21 down on 9 October 1966.

From May 1967 onwards, the MiG count over Vietnam was on the increase but, on the first of the month, Lt-Cdr M. O. Wright of VF-211 managed to bring down a MiG-17 that was intent on shooting down an A-4. Another A-4 and F-8 strike against SAM positions encountered a number of MiGs on 19 May but pilots of VF-24 and VF-211 saw off the attack and four MiGs were shot down for loss of one F-8E of VF-211, which was struck by a SAM. Four more MiG-17s were brought down by the F-8s of VF-24 and VF-211 on 21 July 1967. Commander L. R. Myers achieved the first kill for the F-8H variant on 26 June 1968 when he downed a MiG-21. Between 1966 and 1968, the Crusader was the chief MiG-killer in the region, the last of them on 19 September 1968 when Lt Anthony Nargi of VF-111 'Det 2' shot down a MiG-21. From that day onwards, all further MiG kills would be credited to the F-4 Phantom. The grand total for the F-8 Crusader would stand at nineteen enemy aircraft, made up of sixteen MiG-17s and three MiG-21s.

While the F-8 Crusader is regularly referred to as the 'Last of the Gunfighters', the majority of the type's success during the Vietnam War was achieved with the Sidewinder missile, with the odd exception. Only two Crusader kills were achieved just with guns compared to the F-105, a fighter-bomber, which claimed 24½ kills with its guns! Those two kills appeared to have occurred on the same day: 21 July 1967. That day, Lt Cdr Bob Kirkwood of VF-24 claimed a MiG-17 and Lt Cdr Tim Hubbard of VF-211 also claimed a MiG-17 with cannon, assisted by Zuni rockets! Hubbard also claimed a pair of MiG-17 probables with cannon during the same engagement. The Crusader's 20 mm cannon was prone to jamming during high-G manoeuvres because the ammunition belts would flex and buckle during violent combat, which would result in the weapon failing at the crucial moment.

Only three F-8E Crusaders were actually shot down by MiGs, the first of them, Lieutenant Cole Black's F-8E No. 149152 of VF-211, on 21 June 1966. Black ejected safely but became a

POW soon after and was destined not to be released until 12 February 1973. Commander Dick Bellinger's F-8E was hit by MiGs on 14 July 1966, forcing him to divert to Da Nang. Unfortunately, Bellinger's aircraft ran out of fuel, but he ejected safely over friendly territory. The final F-8E loss was on 5 September 1966 when Captain W. K. Abbot USAF of VF-111 was forced to eject from No. 150896 near Nihn Binh, North Vietnam.

Following the decommissioning of VFP-62 on 5 January 1968, VFP-63 became the only RF-8 unit with enough available aircraft for detachments aboard US Navy carriers. By 1971, VFP-63 was re-organised with a single permanent shore command plus two detachments covering the Atlantic Fleet and three covering the Pacific Fleet. VFP-3 continued to evolve into the core Crusader unit when it took over all F-8 training from 1 September 1972.

In the meantime, 1972 saw a resurgence of hostilities over Vietnam. However, by this time, the F-4 Phantom was the US Navy's primary fighter and the F-8s were relegated to reconnaissance escort and air-to-ground missions.

The USMC Crusaders also played their part in the Vietnam War, VMF(AW)-212 joining USS *Oriskany* in 1965 with one aircraft being lost and its pilot becoming a POW. The bulk of USMC F-8 Crusader operations were actually flown from shore bases, including Da Nang and Chu Lai, the home of VMF(AW)-232 and VMF(AW)-235 from 1966, the former taking part in a number of operations during the North Vietnamese siege of Khe Sanh. The RF-8A was operated by VMCJ-1, which detached its aircraft to a number of carriers until the RF-4B Phantom began to be introduced from October 1966 onwards. This only left the F-8Es of VMF(AW)-232 and -235 in USMC service, of which a dozen were eventually lost to a combination of enemy flak and losses on the ground following rocket attacks against ground bases.

The F-8 Crusader's days as a carrier-based fighter were all but over by 1972 and a rapid relegation to either a reserve unit or storage in the desert had begun. At the end of the Vietnam War, there were just four fighter squadrons remaining in theatre, all operating the F-8J: VF-24 and VF-211 on board the USS *Hancock* and VF-191 and VF-194 on the USS *Oriskany*.

Post-war, only the USS *Hancock* remained in the Gulf of Tonkin but, in October 1973, she was ordered to the Middle East to support the Israeli Defence Forces during the Yom Kippur War. Loaded with A-4 Skyhawks and F-8 Crusaders, the intention was to bolster the IDF with further A-4s, a number of which were already being supplied. In the end, the Israelis did not need the direct support of the USS *Hancock* and she returned to the US instead with a full complement of aircraft.

1976 was the year of the final Crusader cruise, with the aircraft of VF-191 and VF-194 aboard USS *Oriskany*. On its return to the US, USS *Oriskany* was decommissioned and the last of the Crusader fighters were officially withdrawn from service and flown direct to Davis-Monthan AFB. This left the RF-8Gs of VFP-63 as the only Crusaders in US Navy service and, following the departure of the RF-5C Vigilante in 1979, these were the only carrier-based reconnaissance aircraft available. VFP-63 provided a number of detachments for tours of duty in the Persian Gulf and during the Iranian hostage situation. The USS *Coral Sea* hosted the final RF-8G cruise in March 1982 and, in June, VFP-63 was stood down and the RF-8G was retired from US Navy service.

In the reserve, the F-8A and F-8B had been serving since 1965; these particular machines were operated by the US Navy and USMC and, uniquely, wore both markings. Three F-8 Crusader reserve units, VF-661, VF-703 and VF-931, were mobilised in 1968 following the seizure of the intelligence ship USS *Pueblo* by the North Koreans on 5 January of that year. However, twelve months after mobilisation, none of these squadrons had become operational thanks to multiple problems, including maintenance of the early F-8A and

F-8B. By 1970, the situation was rectified when the reserve units were reorganised into a pair of carrier wings; namely CVWR-20 and CVWR-30, the former attached to the Atlantic and the latter to the Pacific Fleet. Equipped with new variants of the Crusader, each wing was made up of eight squadrons, comprising two fighter, three attack, one airborne early warning, a tanker and a single light photo unit. Of this group, the F-8 Crusader equipped the two fighter and light photo squadrons.

Other reserve units included VF-201 and VF-202, operating out of Dallas, and VF-301 and VF-302 stationed at NAS Miramar, all operating the F-8H, which was later replaced by the F-8J. VFP-206 and VFP-306, both based at Andrews AFB, operated the RF-8G which, among other tasks, carried out pre-show photography for the Blue Angels display team. The composite VC-13 was formed at New Orleans in 1973, equipped with the F-8H, although this was to be short-lived as it was replaced by the A-4L within twelve months.

The US Navy and USMC reserve units dispensed with the F-8 in 1975, making way for the F-4B. This left the RF-8G in service, which soldiered on in the reserve with VFP-206 until it was finally retired on 29 March 1987. The last aircraft, RF-8G No. 146860, was presented to the Smithsonian Institution the same day and VFP-206 was deactivated the following day.

The USS *Saratoga's* (CV-60) first deployment to the Mediterranean with the US Sixth Fleet in 1958, with the Crusaders of VF-32 and Demons of VF-31 parked along the flight deck. (*Official US Navy photograph via R. L. Ward Collection*)

Above: Vought F8U-1 Crusader No. 143747 '201/AC' of VF-32 'Fighting Swordsmen' prepares to launch from HMS *Ark Royal*. Not long after this image was taken, the aircraft crashed into the sea off USS *Saratoga* on 25 September 1958. (*R. L. Ward Collection*)

Below: VMF-333 was the first USMC unit to receive the F-8 Crusader in 1960, operating the type until 1966, when it was replaced by the F-4 Phantom. (*R. L. Ward Collection*)

The task of flying low-level, high-speed reconnaissance missions during the Cuban Missile Crisis was carried out by aircraft from the US Navy's VFP-62 and the USMC's VMCJ-2, both operating out of NAS Cecil Field, Florida. (*Official US Navy photograph via R. L. Ward Collection*)

RF-8A Crusader No. 145624 '901' of VFP-2 prepares to take off from USS *Kitty Hawk* for another low-level operation over Laos in 1964. (*R. L. Ward Collection*)

It was an F-8A Crusader of VF-211 'Fighting Checkmates' that claimed the first enemy kill over Vietnam on 12 June 1966. (*Official US Navy photograph via R. L. Ward Collection*)

Above: The catapult officer gives the 'GO' signal to launch an F-8C Crusader of VF-194 from the USS *Ticonderoga* on 14 September 1966. (*Official US Navy via Joseph T. Thompson and via R. L. Ward Collection*)

Below: VF-24 'Red Checkertails' re-equipped with the F-8 Crusader in 1957 and retained the type until 1975 when it was replaced by the F-14 Tomcat. They bagged their first MiG kill over Vietnam on 21 July 1967. (*Official US Navy photograph via R. L. Ward Collection*)

Above: The 'Red Checkertails' displayed in full colour on the tail of this VF-24 F-8C Crusader. (*R. L. Ward Collection*)

Left: No. 145625 was originally built as an RF-8A and is pictured here after conversion to a RF-8G and re-entry into service with VFP-63. Following the decommissioning of VFP-62 on 5 January 1968, VFP-63 became the only remaining RF-8 unit. (*Official US Navy photograph via R. L. Ward Collection*)

Above: F-8E Crusader No. 149191 '9/DB' of VMF(AW)-235, USMC, taxiing at Da Nang or Chu Lai in 1966. (*Official US Navy photograph via R. L. Ward Collection*)

Below: By the end of the Vietnam War only four F-8J Crusader units remained in theatre, including VF-211 operating from USS *Hancock*. (*R. L. Ward Collection*)

Above: 1976 was the year of the final Crusader cruise with the aircraft of VF-191 and VF-194 aboard USS *Oriskany*. F-8J Crusader No. 150238 '206/NM' was placed in storage at the AMARC in March 1976 and ended its days as a target on the Cannon Range, New Mexico. (*R. L. Ward Collection*)

Below: F-8A Crusader No. 143785 of reserve unit VF-661, one of three mobilised following the USS *Pueblo* incident in 1968. (*R. L. Ward Collection*)

Above: Another Crusader reserve unit was VF-201, which operated the F-8H (and later the F-8J) from Dallas. This F-8H was another aircraft which ended its days as a target, on this occasion on the Tolicha Peak Range, Nevada. (*R. L. Ward Collection*)

Below: RF-8G Crusader No. 146855 '604' of VFP-306, based at Andrews AFB. (*R. L. Ward Collection*)

Aéronavale and Philippines Air Force

During the sales tour for the TF-8A trainer, by then nicknamed the 'Twosader', the aircraft made an appearance at the 1962 Paris Air Show. The French were quite taken by the aircraft and were on the hunt for a replacement for the Sud-Est Aquilon (a license-built de Havilland Sea Venom) and nothing 'home-grown' was in the pipeline. That was all fine; however, France's two main aircraft carriers, the *Clemenceau* and *Foch*, were too small for the Crusader to operate from. The solution was to create a new aircraft, designated the F-8E(FN), complete with the same BLC wing as fitted to the F-8J, which allowed them to operate from the smaller French carriers. As mentioned earlier, the BLC was designed to reduce the approach speed of the Crusader; to compensate and to maintain good control at lower speed, the tailplane was enlarged. The standard 20 mm cannon were left in place, as were the four AIM-9B Sidewinder mounts on the forward fuselage. Provision was also in place for a pair of Matra R530 air-to-air missiles on the same forward fuselage mounts. There were two different versions of the R530: an infrared homer and a semi-active radar-homer. A common fit on the F-8E(FN) was to carry one of each, and to support the R530 a Magnavox AN/APQ-104 radar was installed, backed up by an AN/ANG-4 fire control system.

Carrier trials on board the *Clemenceau* were carried out by a pair of VF-32 F-8s in March 1962. The prototype F-8E(FN) was actually F-8D No. 147036, which made its maiden flight on 27 February 1964. The first of forty-two production aircraft flew on 26 June 1964 and deliveries began on 5 October 1964, with the first machines being delivered to Saint Nazaire. It should be noted that these aircraft retained the standard wing and that the new BLC wings were not installed until 1969. Further modifications would include the Matra R550 Magic infrared-homing air-to-air missile in 1973, the installation of the J57-P-20A engine in 1979 and the Magic 2 missile from 1988. Further upgrades to extend the life of the aircraft began in the early 1990s and included a new Martin Baker zero-zero ejection seat, new wiring and hydraulic system, upgraded cockpit instruments, a gyroscopic navigation system and a Thomson-CSF Sherloc RWR. Only seventeen aircraft were selected for the later upgrades, which were designed to keep the aircraft in service for at least another decade and resulted in another new designation, the F-8P (P standing for 'Prolongé').

The F-8(FN) first entered service with Flottille 12 in October 1964 and 14F replaced its piston-powered F4U-7 Corsairs a few months later, in March 1965. The latter unit was re-equipped with the Étendard in 1979, which left 12F to soldier on for much longer than planned. In fact, the Aéronavale Crusaders were destined to become the last examples of the type in service and were not replaced by the Rafale M until 2000.

The only other air arm to operate the Crusader was the Philippines Air Force, who purchased thirty-five ex-US Navy F-8Hs in late 1977. Twenty-five of this batch, which had been in open storage at Davis-Monthan AFB, would be refurbished by Vought, while the remainder served as replacement/spares machines. Vought were also tasked with training the Filipino pilots and for this they utilised the sole TF-8A, only for it to be lost after a few months. The Crusader entered Philippines Air Force service with the 7th TFS, 5th FW, stationed at Basa in place of the seriously obsolete F-86F Sabre. Apart from local defensive duties, the Crusaders were also used to intercept Soviet bombers; however, it was not long before serviceability issues began to creep in. Those Crusaders that were airworthy were temporarily relocated to Clark AFB on Luzon Island during the demise of President Ferdinand Marcos in 1986 due to the threat of sabotage. The remaining aircraft did not last much longer. The type was phased out on 23 January 1988 and, following damage caused by the eruption of Mount Pinatubo, were withdrawn in 1991.

Designated the F-8E(FN), the Aéronavale Crusader was completed with the same BLC wing as fitted to the F-8J, which allowed them to operate from the smaller French carriers. (*R. L. Ward Collection*)

A-4C Skyhawk No. 147826 refuels Aéronavale F-8E (FN) Crusader '4' during its delivery flight to France on 14 October 1964. (*Official US Navy photograph (PAP 13703-10-64) via R. L. Ward Collection*)

F-8E(FN) '38' of Flottille 12 pictured in 1975. On 1 March 1978 the aircraft crashed on landing at Flottille 12's home airfield at Landivisiau AB, Brittany. (*R. L. Ward Collection*)

F-8E(FN) Crusader '37' of Flottille 12 during a visit to Yeovilton. Later converted to an F-8P, the aircraft was DBR during an engine test at Cuers AB, Provence. (*R. L. Ward Collection*)

One of the thirty-five ex-US Navy F-8Hs purchased for the Philippine Air Force in 1978, destined to serve for just a decade. (*R. L. Ward Collection*)

The Crusader III

Born in 1955 and designed and developed in direct competition with the McDonnell F4H-1 Phantom (later McDonnell Douglas F-4 Phantom II), the XF8U-3 Crusader III was an incredible aircraft. While it bore some resemblance to the F-8, the Crusader III was a completely different animal. The dimensions and weights, not to mention a more powerful 29,000 lb (wet) Pratt & Whitney J75-P-5A engine, set the Crusader III apart. In appearance, the aircraft had a dramatic forward-raked air intake and large ventral fins which were extended in flight. Regarding armament, internal guns were dispensed with and an all-missile arrangement was made up of a trio of AIM-7 Sparrows or four AIM-9 Sidewinders.

The first of three prototypes, No. 146340, carried out its maiden flight in the hands of John Konrad on 2 June 1958, just six days after the Phantom. From the outset, the Crusader III was an amazing performer and, during early flight testing, was clocked at speeds in the region of Mach 2.2. It could carry out a zoom climb to a remarkable 90,000 ft while sustaining altitudes of between 60,000 and 65,000 ft could be achieved with ease. The aircraft was not perfect but, with further development time, could have been a winner. However, the US Navy preferred the twin-seat, twin-engine arrangement of the F-4 Phantom and the rest is history.

Only three XF8U-3 Crusader IIIs were built and, following the cancellation of the programme, all three were allocated to NASA along with a fourth part-built airframe for spares support. Sadly, all three of these exotic and unusual aircraft were eventually scrapped.

The first of three XF8U-3 Crusader III prototypes, No. 146340, which carried out its maiden flight in the hands of John Konrad on 2 June 1958. (*Chance Vought/LTV via R. L. Ward Collection*)

In appearance, the XF8U-3 Crusader III had dramatic forward-raked air intake and large ventral fins which were extended in flight, as demonstrated here. (*Chance Vought/ LTV via R. L. Ward Collection*)

An incredible performer capable of over Mach 2.2, the Crusader III lost out to the twin-engined, twin-crew F-4 Phantom. (*Chance Vought/LTV via R. L. Ward Collection*)

The Crusader could carry out a zoom climb to a remarkable 90,000 ft while sustaining altitudes of between 60,000 and 65,000 ft. (*Chance Vought/ LTV via R. L. Ward Collection*)

F-8 Crusader Technical Information

F-8 Crusader Engine

Type	Powerplant
XF8U-1	10,900 lb (Dry), 14,500 lb (Wet) Pratt & Whitney J57-P-11 Turbojet
F8U-1 (F-8A)	10,000 lb (Dry), 16,200 lb (Wet) J57-P-12A
	10,000 lb (Dry), 16,200 lb (Wet) J57-P-4A/-12
F8U-1P (RF-8A)	10,000 lb (Dry), 16,200 lb (Wet) J57-P-4A/-12
RF-8G	10,700 lb (Dry), 17,000 lb (Wet) J57-P-22
	11,000 lb (Dry), 19,500 lb (Wet) J57-P-429
F8U-1E (F-8B)	10,000 lb (Dry), 16,200 lb (Wet) J57-P-4A/-12
F8U-2 (F-8C)	10,700 lb (Dry), 16,900 lb (Wet) J57-P-16
F8U-2N (F-8D)	10,700 lb (Dry), 18,000 lb (Wet) J57-P-20
F8U-2NE (F-8E) and (FN)	10,700 lb (Dry), 18,000 lb (Wet) J57-P-20A
F8U-1T (TF-8A)	10,000 lb (Dry), 16,200 lb (Wet) J57-P-20 'de-rated'
F-8H/J/K and L	10,700 lb (Dry), 18,000 lb (Wet) J57-P-20A
XF8U-3	16,500 lb (Dry), 29,500 lb (Wet) J75-P-5A/6

F-8 Crusader Performance (mph, Mach and feet)

Type	Max Speed	Cruise	Climb Rate	Service Ceiling	Combat Range (Max)
XF8U-1	At least Mach 1	-	-	-	-
F8U-1 (F-8A)	1,013 mph (Mach 1.53)	570 mph	20,000 ft/pm	42,300 ft	1,474 miles
RF-8G	1,190 mph (Mach 1.8)	-	-	41,600 ft	640*
F8U-1E (F-8B)	1,013 mph (Mach 1.53)	570 mph	20,000 ft/pm	42,300 ft	1,474 miles
F8U-2 (F-8C)	1,105 mph (Mach 1.67)	570 mph	21,700 ft/pm	41,700 ft	1,490 miles
F8U-2N (F-8D)	1,228 mph (Mach 1.86)	570 mph	-	42,900 ft	1,737 miles (guns only)
F8U-2NE (F-8E)	1,133 mph (Mach 1.72)	570 mph	27,200 ft/pm	59,000 ft	1,425 miles
F-8H	1,020 mph (Mach 1.55)	-	-	-	-
F-8J	1,086 mph (Mach 1.65)	551 mph	-	47,800 ft**	1,576 miles
XF8U-3	1,457 mph (Mach 2.21)	575 mph	32,500 ft/pm	60,000 ft	2,044 miles***

*Combat radius
**Combat ceiling
***Not combat

F-8 Crusader Weights (all pounds)

Type	Empty	Combat	Gross	Max Take-Off
F8U-1 (F-8A)	15,513	23,659	26,961	27,468
RF-8G	17,300	-	-	27,822
F8U-2 (F-8C)	16,483	24,347	27,810	27,938
F8U-2N (F-8D)	17,541	25,098	28,765	29,000
F8U-2NE (F-8E)	17,836	28,000	34,100	-
F-8H	18,700	-	29,200	-
F-8J/K and L	19,751	30,352	31,318	36,587
XF8U-3	21,862	32,318	37,856	38,772

F-8 Crusader Dimensions (feet and inches)

Type	Span	Length	Height	Wing Area
F8U-1 (F-8A)	35 ft 8 in.	54 ft 3 in.	15 ft 9 in.	375 sq/ft
F8U-1E (F-8B)	35 ft 8 in.	54 ft 3 in.	15 ft 9 in.	375 sq/ft
F8U-2 (F-8C)	35 ft 8 in.	54 ft 3 in.	15 ft 9 in.	375 sq/ft
F8U-2N (F-8D)	35 ft 8 in.	54 ft 3 in.	15 ft 9 in.	375 sq/ft
F8U-2NE (F-8E)	35 ft 2 in.	54 ft 6 in.	15 ft 9 in.	350 sq/ft
F-8H	35 ft 8 in.	54 ft 3 in.	15 ft 9 in.	375 sq/ft
F-8JK and L	35 ft 8 in.	54 ft 6 in.	15 ft 9 in.	350 sq/ft
XF8U-3	38 ft 11 in.	58 ft 8 in.	16 ft 4 in.	450sq/ft

F-8 Crusader Armament/External Stores

F8U-1 (F-8A)
4 x 20 mm Colt-Browning Mk 12 cannon with 144 rpg and 2 x AIM-9A Sidewinders
Rocket pack carrying 32 2.75 in. FFAR rockets

F8U-1P (RF-8A)
Nil*

RF-8G
Nil*

F8U-1E (F-8B)
4 x 20 mm Colt-Browning Mk 12 cannon with 144 rpg and 2 x AIM-9A Sidewinders
Rocket pack carrying 32 2.75 in. FFAR rockets

F8U-2 (F-8C)
4 x 20 mm Colt-Browning Mk 12 cannon with 144 rpg and 2 x AIM-9A Sidewinders
Rocket pack carrying 32 2.75 in. FFAR rockets

F8U-2N (F-8D)
4 x 20 mm Colt-Browning Mk 12 cannon with 144 rpg and 2 x AIM-9A Sidewinders

F8U-2NE (F-8E)
4 x 20 mm Colt-Browning Mk 12 cannon with 144 rpg and 4 x AIM-9A Sidewinders 4,000 lb of bombs or rockets on underwing pylons in the following combinations: 12 x 250 lb bombs, 8 x 500 lb bombs or 4 x 1,000 lb bombs and/or 8 x Zuni unguided air-to-surface rockets or 2 x AGM-12A or AGM-12B Bullpup missiles

F-8E (FN)
4 x 20 mm Colt-Browning Mk 12 cannon. A progression of the Matra R530, occasionally the AIM-9B Sidewinder, Matra Super 530 and the Matra R550 Magic

F8U-1T (TF-8A)
2 x 20 mm Colt-Browning Mk 12 cannon

F-8H
4 x 20 mm Colt-Browning Mk 12 cannon with 144 rpg and 4 x AIM-9A Sidewinders

F-8J, K and L
4 x 20 mm Colt-Browning Mk 12 cannon with 144 rpg and 4 x AIM-9A Sidewinders. Provision for a pair of 300-gallon drop tanks and/or capable of carrying 5,000 lb of bombs or rockets

XF8U-3
Projected: 3 x AIM-7 Sparrow and 4 x AIM-9 Sidewinder

*Sidewinder rails were fitted

The Ling-Temco-Vought A-7 Corsair Story

'Scooter' Replacement

Having first entered service four years earlier, the US Navy began looking for a new strike aircraft to replace the Douglas A-4 Skyhawk in 1960. Nicknamed the 'Scooter', the A-4 was a popular aircraft but the US Navy wanted a machine that could deliver a bigger payload over a longer range. Ironically, the A-4 would outlive its 'replacement' by some margin and was not fully retired from US Navy service until 2003!

Some time was lost looking at an aircraft capable of supersonic speed, but it was soon realised that little would be gained, especially at low level carrying an array of external stores. As a result, the remit shifted to a subsonic aircraft and a specification for a 'VA(L)' (Light Attack Aircraft) was issued. The specification included the use of a Pratt & Whitney TF30 bypass turbojet, two 20 mm cannon, the capability to carry up to 12,000 lb of ordnance, a combat radius of 690 miles and a radar and capability to operate in all weather conditions. Initially, all eyes focussed on Douglas, who quickly drew up a TF-30-powered version of the A-4 Skyhawk designated the A4D-6. This favouritism towards Douglas was somewhat frowned upon by other US aircraft manufacturers and the US Navy had no other choice than to throw the specification out there for everyone to compete over. To keep development costs down, the new strike aircraft would have to be based upon an existing design. The competition was between Douglas, Grumman, North American and LTV. The Grumman design, the G-128-12, was effectively a single-seat version of the A-6 Intruder while the North American NA-295 was similar to the FJ-4 Fury. The LTV design, designated the V-463, was effectively a ground attack version of the F-8 Crusader, on paper at least. Utilising as many F-8 parts as possible at the stage of its development, the commonality would slowly reduce as the aircraft evolved but the US Navy was completely sold and, despite deviating from the original remit by some margin, the LTV design was announced as the winner on 11 February 1964. On 19 March, LTV was awarded a contract for seven flight test/pre-production aircraft and thirty-five production machines, to be allocated the US Navy designation A-7.

A Passing Resemblance

The configuration adopted by LTV was well-suited to ground attack operations, especially at a healthy subsonic speed. The wing had a moderate sweep and the all-important underwing pylons, of which there were six, were roughly in line so as to reduce the pitching motion when the weapon was released. Two further pylons were attached to the fuselage flanks to the rear of the cockpit, under the leading edge of the wing, for a pair of self-defence air-to-air missiles. There was also a slight taper to the wing and the leading edge had a small extension to reduce the tendency to tip-stall, which would have reduced the aircraft's manoeuvrability.

The wing was positioned high on the fuselage, allowing for a natural amount of ground clearance when large underwing stores were carried. The tailplane was located lower than the main wing, which all but eliminated the chances of pitching up. The height of the main fin compared to the F-8 was reduced in an effort to save space when hangered below deck, while the basic configuration of the air intake was similar to the Crusader, but that just about sums up the similarities.

One of the features that the US Navy was most likely expecting was the F-8's variable-incidence wing. However, this was replaced by a more traditional fixed wing with a steeper deck angle attitude and the installation of bigger flaps. The powerful, thirsty J57 afterburning turbojet was replaced by the comparatively frugal 11,350 lb Pratt & Whitney TF30-P-6 non-afterburning turbofan. Internal armament, on the early variants at least, consisted of a pair of 20 mm Mk 12 cannon as per the F-8 with 600 rpg, positioned in the lower forward fuselage. Later variants would carry a single internal gun, although this was a powerful one, a 20 mm M61VA1 six-barrel cannon with space for up to 1,000 rounds.

Early aircraft would also be equipped with a Texas Instruments AN/APQ-116 Multi-Mode Terrain Following Radar, an ILAAS (Integrated Light Attack Avionics System) which operated by combining Doppler-inertial navigation and a central digital computer plus a Lear-Siegler autopilot. These were very state-of-the-art, incredibly complex systems which needed to be accessed quickly and easily as the US Navy had also specified that the aircraft should not exceed 11.5 maintenance hours per hour of flight time, a very low figure at the time. Easy and efficient maintenance was at the forefront of the design and, as such, the aircraft had no less than thirty-five access panels, which equated to almost 50 per cent of the aircraft's entire surface area! Early variants also had the ability to refuel mid-air (using the probe and drogue method) thanks to a retractable boom housed in the starboard side of the forward fuselage.

The US Navy was under a great deal of pressure to reach the best deal so the maintainability and delivery schedule and the aircraft empty weight were subject to penalty clauses should they be breached. In the end, Vought only had to pay out for going over the empty weight by 600 lb (4 per cent): the aircraft should have weighed in at 14,857 lb according to the original contract.

Well Ahead of Schedule

A mere seventeen months after the original contract was signed, the first YA-7A-1CV was rolled out on 13 August 1965 and, a few weeks later, the prototype, serial No. 152580, carried out its maiden flight with John Konrad in the cockpit on 27 September. This incredible achievement almost halved the expected development time for such a complex military aircraft and, on top of that, the prototype was airborne twenty-five days ahead of the official schedule. The US Navy raised its order by another 140 aircraft on 10 November 1965 and, the same day, the aircraft was officially christened the Corsair II in honour of their most famous aircraft to date, the Second World War Corsair fighter. This was some name to carry at the time but LTV was confident that the Corsair II would be as good an aircraft as its older sibling. In service, a more 'affectionate' name was applied to the A-7: SLUF, short for 'Short Little Ugly Fella', although the 'Fella' was more often replaced by a slightly cruder word!

The original contract also stated that delivery should begin by 1967 and this was achieved by LTV when the first A-7s were delivered to VA-174 and VA-122, both fleet readiness squadrons, in September and October 1966 respectively. The first carrier qualifications were carried out on USS *America* on 15 November 1966 while the very first A-7A operational unit, VA-147, was commissioned on 1 February 1967. BIS (Board of Inspection & Survey) and FIP (Fleet Introduction Programme) trials were fully complied with on 1 June 1967 and, by the autumn of 1967, VA-147 began taking delivery of fully combat-ready A-7As.

Above: The first of three YA-7A-1CV Corsair II prototypes, No. 152580 at Dallas, which first flew on 27 September 1965, just seventeen months after the initial contract was signed. The aircraft was destroyed at NAF China Lake on 23 March 1966, the pilot ejecting safely. (*LTV (A. L. Schoeni) via Joseph T. Thompson via R. L. Ward Collection*)

Below: Early production A-7A Corsair II No. 152650 during steam catapult trials at the Naval Air Test Facility at NAS Lakehurst, New Jersey, on 1 January 1967. (*Official US Navy photograph (25165) via R. L. Ward Collection*)

Visual proof that the A-7 Corsair II light attack bomber was designed from the beginning for maintainability and serviceability is amply furnished in this photograph. (*LTV via R. L. Ward Collection*)

The first A-7A Corsair IIs were delivered to VA-174 and VA-122 in September and October 1966. This aircraft, No. 153169, served with the former. (*R. L. Ward Collection*)

A-7A Corsair II No. 152665 '202/ NJ' of VA-122 flying over Yuma, Arizona, on 14 December 1966. (*Official US Navy Photograph (MAL-17042-12-66) via R. L. Ward Collection*)

Left: An A-7A Corsair II during a test flight carrying single wing pylons loaded with a dozen Mk 12 Snakeye bombs. (*LTV (PR.6651) via R. L. Ward Collection*)

Below: An A-7A Corsair II of the NATC 'Flight Test Division' aboard the USS *America* for carrier qualifications in November 1966. (*Official US Navy photograph (111907) via R L Ward Collection*)

Carrier qualifications continuing onboard the USS *America*, this time in full colour. (*Via R. L. Ward Collection*)

Vought F4U-4 Corsair *Lancer Two* with an A-7A Corsair II of VX-5 tucked in behind. Considering the original Corsair was the 02U back in 1926, the A-7 version should have been named the Corsair III. (*Official US Navy photograph via R. L. Ward Collection*)

Mark by Mark

A-7A

199 production A-7As were built; it was an aircraft that proved to be more durable in combat, to have a much longer range and to be considerably easier to maintain compared to the A-4 Skyhawk. It was not all rosy for the A-7A; the aircraft had an alarming habit of ingesting a large amount of steam during a catapult launch, which caused a dramatic reduction in thrust. This resulted in the A-7A operating with a much lighter weapons load (it was supposed to be 15,000 lb). This problem was later rectified by changing the twelve compressor stage of the engine. The early A-7As only carried 250 rpg for each of their 20 mm Mk 12 cannon. As well as the AN/APQ-115 radar, the A-7A was equipped with an AN/APN-153 navigational radar and an AN/APQ-99 radar.

A-7B

The main difference over the A-7A for this mark was the powerplant, which was upgraded to a 12,200 lb TF30-P-8, which by 1971 was itself superseded by the 13,400 lb TF30-P-408.

Other modifications included improved flaps and upgrading the terrain-following radar to AN/APQ-116 standard.

The first A-7B, No. 154363, made its maiden flight, with Joe Engle in the cockpit, on 6 February 1968. 196 A-7Bs were built, the last of them delivered in May 1969.

A-7C

The original designation A-7C was allocated to a two-seat trainer variant of the A-7B which never left the drawing board; instead, the US Navy ordered the TA-4J Skyhawk. In the meantime, the USAF had placed an order for the Allison TF41-A-1 (a license-built Rolls-Royce Spey), which would be designated as the A-7D. The US Navy was also keen on operating their own TF-41-A-1 version, which was to be designated as the A-7E. As is often the case, airframe development can easily streak ahead of engine development and Allison was falling behind producing its version of the Spey engine. As a result, the first batch of sixty-seven production 'A-7Es' were actually powered by the TF30-P-8 engine and were designated the A-7C. Apart from the engine, the aircraft was produced to 'E' standard, which included a number of improvements such as an HUD, an upgraded avionics package and a single M61 cannon as per the A-7D.

The first A-7C, serialled 156734, first flew on 25 November 1968 with Robert Rostine at the controls. VA-122 a training unit based at NAS Lemoore, California, was the first to receive the type in July 1969, followed by VA-82 'Marauders' and VA-86, both of which were operational units.

A-7D

A mere three months after the maiden flight of the A-7A, the USAF decided that its latest tactical fighter would be a version of the Corsair II. This decision was influenced by the US Army which, at the time, was not allowed to operate fixed-wing combat aircraft but still needed the close support that such a machine could provide. As a result, the USAF went hunting for a specialised subsonic aircraft for the task rather than a more traditional supersonic machine. The A-7 seemed to tick all the necessary boxes but the USAF was not very keen to take on an aircraft that was designed for the US Navy. However, following government pressure, it was announced on 5 November 1965 that the USAF had placed an order for a variant of the Corsair II, to be designated the A-7D.

The specification demanded by the USAF raised the A-7 to a new level, beginning with the installation of the aforementioned 14,500 lb Allison TF41-A-1 turbofan, an engine which was 2,000 lb more powerful than the original TF-30. As per the A-7C, the 'D' variant was fitted with a new HUD, much improved avionics and, in place of the twin 20 mm cannon, a single powerful M61A1 Vulcan rotary cannon with 1,000 rounds. The navigation radar was upgraded to the AN/APN-185 and the terrain-following radar was replaced with the improved AN/APQ-116. Another unique feature of the A-7D was its air-to-air refuelling system. The first twenty-six A-7Ds built retained the same retractable refuelling boom as the early US Navy marks; however, the remainder had a universal air-refuelling receptacle on the upper spine of the aircraft which could receive fuel from the boom of a KC-135 Stratotanker. The latter method would also appear on all later variants of the A-7.

There were three YA-7D prototypes built, although the first two, Nos 14582 and 14583, were installed with a TF30-P-6 engine, the former making its maiden flight on 6 April 1968. The third prototype YA-7D, No. 14584, was the first to be installed with the Allison TF-41 and this took to the air on 26 September 1968.

459 A-7Ds were constructed. The type initially served within three Tactical Air Command Wings and a pair of ANG (Air National Guard) squadrons.

A-7E

The US Navy liked what it saw in the USAF A-7D; in particular, the additional power offered by the Allison TF41 turbofan. As covered by the A-7C scenario, the first production A-7Es had the original TF30-P-5 engine and it was not until 9 March 1969 that the first TF41-A-2-powered A-7E first flew. The only external difference between an A-7D and an A-7E was that the latter retained its retractable refuelling boom while, on the inside, the differences were inside the cockpit. The A-7E had an AN/APN-190 navigation radar and an AN/APQ-129 terrain-following radar. Further upgrades were destined to follow, including the installation of a Texas Instruments AN/AAR-45 FLIR pod which was introduced in 1979 to aid flying both at night and in poor weather conditions.

529 A-7Es were built and the last of them was not delivered to the US Navy until 1983.

YA-7F

Still yet to be fully proven over the battlefield, the spotlight was on the A-10A Thunderbolt II in 1985 to such a degree that the USAF went hunting for a replacement. The USAF issued a proposal for a machine called the Close Air Support/Battlefield Interdictor (CAS/BAI). LTV was not shy in coming forward and quickly proposed a new, supersonic version of the A-7.

LTV received a contract from the USAF on 7 May 1987 to convert a pair of A-7D airframes (Nos 70-1039 and 71-0344). These were initially designated the A-7D Plus before becoming the YA-7F. Power was provided by a single 26,000 lb (with afterburner) F100-PW-220 turbofan, and to accommodate this large engine, the fuselage was extended by 4 feet, which was achieved by installing a pair of plugs fore (30 in.) and aft (18 in.) of the wing. The fin, rudder and flaps were all enlarged and automatic manoeuvring flaps and leading edge wing root extensions were installed. The longer fuselage, which made the aircraft look very similar to the F-8 Crusader, made room for additional fuel. The cockpit was, as you would expect, state of the art and included HOTAS and HUD displays, low altitude night attack systems and much more being development specifically for the YA-7F, which had already gained the appropriate name 'Strikefighter'.

The first prototype YA-7F, No. 71-0344, performed its maiden flight on 29 November 1989 in the hands of Jim Read. A truly impressive performer, Read took the YA-7F through the sound barrier on its second flight. The second YA-7F, No. 70-1039, first flew on 3 April 1990; however, by this time the world stage was changing and the A-10 began to make a name for itself, resulting in the project being cancelled.

A-7G

The first potential overseas variant, the A-7G, was intended for service with the Swiss Air Force. The Swiss were looking for a replacement for their ageing (although not over-worked!) de Havilland Venom FB.50 and FB.54s. The A-7 was chosen because it could deliver a bigger bomb load from a longer slant range with considerably greater accuracy than any of its competitors. However, is it quite possible that politics prevailed and the much cheaper F-5E Tiger II was selected, entering service in 1978, while the Venom soldiered on in the reconnaissance role until 1987 and the F-5 remains in service, albeit in limited numbers.

A-7H and TA-7H

The next version of the Corsair II finally brought overseas sales success in the shape of the A-7H. The customer was the Greek (Hellenic) Air Force (Elliniki Polimiki Aeroporia), which ordered sixty-five aircraft, sixty of which were effectively a land-based version of the A-7E, minus an air-to-air refuelling capability, while the remaining five were TA-7H two-seat trainers. The first A-7H, No. 159662, took to the air on 6 May 1975 and not long afterwards the first examples were serving with 115 Pteriga Mahis (115th Combat Wing), made up of 340 'Alepou' and 345 'Lailaps' Squadrons (A-7 Conversion Unit) at Souda AB, Crete, in place of the long-serving F-84F Thunderstreak. The type is also believed to have served briefly with 338 'Ares' Squadron before it converted to the F-4 Phantom.

Known in Greek service as the 'Koursaro', the type also served with 347 Squadron at Larissa AB from July 1992, during which time the Greeks decided to purchase a second batch of aircraft, made up of fifty former A-7Es and eighteen TA-7Cs, between 1993 and 1994. These aircraft served with the 116 Pteriga Mahis (116th Combat Wing) at Araxos, made up of 335 'Tigreis' and 336 'Olympus' Squadrons in place of the F-104G Starfighter.

The A-7 served the Greek Air Force primarily in the ground attack role but, with the capability to carry a pair of Sidewinders, also carried out air defence duties. Many upgrades were implemented over the years, including improving the thrust of the TF41 engine and continual upgrades to radar and avionics. The 'Koursaro' was popular with both its pilots and groundcrew and was finally retired on 17 October 2014.

TA-7C

The very first production TF41-powered A-7E, No. 156801, was selected for conversion into a two-seat combat-capable trainer/demonstrator in 1972 as a private venture by LTV. The front cockpit would serve for the student pilot while the rear was for the instructor. To achieve this conversion, once again the fuselage needed to be extended, and this was achieved thanks to a 34-inch-long plug inserted in front of the leading edge of the wing. Just like the sole TF-8A, the rear instructor's seat was positioned much higher, making the aircraft look a little hump-backed.

Initially redesignated the YA-7H, No. 156801 first flew on 19 August 1972 in the hands of John Konrad. The designation YA-7H was applied because, at the time, the next available production suffix was 'H', but as we now know this suffix was reserved for the Greek Air Force machines and, instead, the aircraft was redesignated the YA-7E.

The US Navy was obviously impressed with the aircraft and not long after a contract to convert sixty TF-30-powered aircraft was awarded to Vought. The order was made up of twenty-four A-7Bs and thirty-six A-7Cs, all of which would be known as the TA-7C. The first of the order to fly took to the air on 17 December 1976 and was delivered to the US Navy's VA-122 and VA-174 from 31 January 1977.

In 1984, forty-one TA-7Cs were upgraded with an Allison TF41-A-402 engine, making them of a similar standard to the A-7E. The Stencel ejection seat was replaced by the McDonnell Douglas Escapac ejection seat and manoeuvring flaps were installed.

A-7K

Another conversion contract was won by LTV in 1979 when they were tasked to convert an A-7D into a TA-7D. Like the TA-7C, this aircraft was a two-seat advanced trainer, converted in a similar fashion. Once again, it was fully operational and would later be redesignated the A-7K.

The actual production order for thirty aircraft, unlike the TA-7C, were new builds. The first of them were delivered to the ANG in 1981. All of them were destined to serve with ANG units; the last of them were delivered in September 1984.

A-7P

LTV's second export customer was the Força Aérea Portuguesa (FAP) (Portuguese Air Force (PoAF)), which placed an order for twenty aircraft in May 1980. These were to be designated as the A-7P and were ex-US Navy A-7A airframes which would be upgraded with TF30-P-408 engines and avionics from the A-7D and A-7E. The first nine A-7Ps were delivered to Portugal on 24 December 1981 and the type went on to serve with Esc. 302 'Aguisa Reais' and 304 'Magnificos', operating out of Monte Real (Air Base No. 5). However, the official delivery of the A-7P took place at Andrews AFB on 18 August 1981. The twentieth A-7P was delivered on 29 September 1982 and, as well as an additional three airframes for spares, a single TA-7C (No. 154404, nicknamed *Pomba Branca* ('White Dove')) was loaned to the FAP until June 1985.

After renegotiating the original contract in 1983, the Portuguese placed a second order for a further twenty-four A-7Ps and half a dozen A-7As converted to TA-7P standard. The first aircraft of this second batch of twenty-four were delivered between 8 October 1984 and 30 April 1986. However, only twenty-three made it in the end after one of the aircraft was involved in an accident in the US.

Esc. 302 operated the A-7P until 1996 while Esc. 304 continued until 10 June 1999, by which time the type had been superseded by the F-16 Fighting Falcon. A number of aircraft had been lost in flying accidents and, as the type grew older, maintenance became an issue; nonetheless, the Portuguese Corsairs still managed to accumulate 63,600 flying hours during their eighteen-year-long career with the FAP.

EA-7L

On 1 March 1983, a new Tactical Electronic Warfare Squadron, VAQ-34 ('Flashbacks'), was formed at the Pacific Missile Test Center at Point Mugu, California. The unit's responsibility was to train US Navy ship crews to deal with the Soviet electronic and cruise-missile threats. The unit had to find its own aircraft and many of them, such as the RA-3B Skywarrior, were recovered from the Davis-Monthan AFB boneyard and then reconverted to suit the task ahead by the personnel of VAQ-34. The same applied to a small batch of TA-7C Corsair IIs which were 'acquired/transferred' from various units across the fleet. Modification work to turn these A-7s into electronic aggressor aircraft was also carried out at Point Mugu and, once completed, the aircraft emerged as the EA-7L. The modifications included jamming pods and missile simulators, all of which were carried on the underwing pylons. While VAQ-134 records claim that six aircraft were converted to EA-7L standard, the unit actually operated seven along with a couple of TA-7Cs.

When Vought carried out its 1984 upgrade of the TA-7C fleet, the EA-7Ls were included and were fitted with the Allison TF41-A-402 engine. All of the avionics were also brought up to A-7E standard. By 1991, the Skywarrior and Corsair II fleet had been retired from VAQ-34 and the F/A-18A Hornet had taken over.

The pilot of A-7A Corsair '15/XE' of VX-5 (Air Development Squadron 5) gives us a wave while operating out of NAS China Lake, California. (*Official US Navy photograph via R. L. Ward Collection*)

Above: A-7A Corsair II No. 153194 of VA-105 preparing to depart NAS Cecil Field, Florida. This aircraft enjoyed a second career as an A-7P with the Portuguese Air Force. (*Official US Navy photograph via R. L. Ward Collection*)

Below: A-7A Corsair II No. 153261 '311/AE' of VA-82 on final approach to land on USS *America* on 3 February 1968. (*Official US Navy photograph (CVA-66 1212) via R. L. Ward Collection*)

A-7B Corsair II No. 154476 '511/AH' of VA-25 operating from USS *Ticonderoga*. This aircraft is still serving on the gate at NAS El Centro, California. (*Official US Navy Photograph via R. L. Ward Collection*)

A-7B Corsair II No. 154531 '407/NE' of VA-56 (USS *Ranger*) based at NAS Lemoore, California, is pictured over a bombing range in southern California with a load of bombs on its centre wing pylons. This image was captured by Lt Gardener Gray, flying an RF-8G of VFP-63. (*Official US Navy photograph via R. L. Ward Collection*)

A lovely study of A-7B-4-CV Corsair II No. 154536 '405/NE' of VA-56 (USS *Ranger*). The aircraft later became one of twenty-four A-7Bs converted to the two-seat TA-7C. (*Official US Navy photograph via R. L. Ward Collection*)

65

Above: A-7B Corsair II No. 154488 'AC' of VA-46 is 'manhandled' into position for the catapult of USS *Saratoga* in November 1969. (*Official US Navy photograph via R. L. Ward Collection*)

Below: LTV A-7C-1-CV Corsair II No. 156736, one of the original TF30-powered batch of sixty-seven A-7Es which were actually designated as A-7Cs, about to launch from USS *Independence*. (*Official US Navy photograph via R. L. Ward Collection*)

Above: A-7C Corsair II No. 156755 '303/AJ' of VA-82 'Marauders' on board USS *America*. (*R. L. Ward Collection*)

Below: The prototype YA-7D-1-CV Corsair II, No. 67-14582, which carried out its maiden flight on 6 April 1968. (*LTV (PR.8688) via R. L. Ward Collection*)

Above: The third prototype YA-7D-1CV Corsair II, No. 67-14584, loaded with eight 750 lb Mk 117 bombs during early flight testing. (*LTV (PR.8879) via R. L. Ward Collection*)

Below: With test pilot John Konrad at the controls, this A-7D is being used to practice heavy-load (12,500 lb bomb load) inflight refuelling from a USAF KC-135. (*TSgt George Alvarado USAF via R. L. Ward Collection*)

Major Robert Lilac, the project officer for hot and cold weather tests, at the controls of an A-7D during refuelling under extreme cold conditions over Alaska. Further weather tests were flown over Panama and Arizona. (*USAF (S/Sgt Miglionico) via R. L. Ward Collection*)

YA-7D-1-CV Corsair II No. 67-14582 taxies out for flight test at LTV's plant at Dallas. (*LTV (A. L. Schoeni) via R. L. Ward Collection*)

VA-192 'Golden Dragons' (USS *Kitty Hawk*) A-7E Corsair II No. 157530 '300/NH', which was brought down by AAA over North Vietnam on 2 November 1972. (*LTV via R. L. Ward Collection*)

Effectively the US Navy's version of the USAF's A-7D, the A-7E Corsair II was a real workhorse, playing a significant role in the Vietnam War. (*Official US Navy photograph via R. L. Ward Collection*)

The YA-7F 'Strikefighter' (A-7D+) had the look of an F-8 Crusader thanks to its stretched fuselage. (*LTV via R. L. Ward Collection*)

Above: Greek Air Force A-7H Corsair II No. 159938, one of sixty-five ordered, the last of them not retiring until 2014. (*R. L. Ward Collection*)

Below: The first TA-7H Corsair II delivered to the Greek Air Force was No. 161219. (*R. L. Ward Collection*)

Above: VA-174 TA-7C Corsair IIs No. 156767 '372/AD' and No. 156789 '370/AD'; the two-seat configuration suited the A-7 well. (*LTV via R. L. Ward Collection*)

Below: The US Navy ordered twenty-four single-seat A-7Bs and thirty-six A-7Cs to be converted to TA-7C standard, including No. 156773 '217/NJ' of VA-122 (USS *Lexington*). (*R. L. Ward Collection*)

The first A-7D
conversion to
A-K standard was
No. 73-008, which
was designated as
the YA-7K Corsair II.
The aircraft is
pictured in service
with the Arizona
ANG. (*USAF via
R. L. Ward Collection*)

Ease of maintenance
was one of the
many initial criteria
of the A-7 Corsair
and this ANG A-7K
displays some of the
thirty-five available
access panels.
(*'Mil-Slides' Surry via
'Omega1108'*)

The Força Aérea
Portuguesa (FAP)
(Portuguese Air Force
(PoAF)) operated
the A-7P Corsair II
between 1981 and
1999. (*R. L. Ward
Collection*)

Four 'electronic aggressor' aircraft of VAQ-134, beginning with a TA-7C (later converted to an EA-7L) in the foreground, a pair of EA-7Ls and a Douglas ERA-3B in the distance. (*Official US Navy photograph via R. L. Ward Collection*)

Other Operators

While the A-7H and the A-7P were produced specifically for the use of Greece and Portugal, one other operator purchased A-7s 'off the shelf'. This was the Royal Thai Navy Air Arm (Kong Tup Rua Thai or Ratchanavee Thai), who purchased a batch of fourteen refurbished (drawn from AMARC) A-7Es and four TA-7Cs specifically for coastal defence and sea patrol missions. Following removal from Davis-Monthan, the aircraft were extensively inspected and repaired at NAS Jacksonville, Florida, before delivery commenced in mid-1995. The aircraft served with the 10th 'White Shark' Squadron, 1st Wing, based at U-Tapao Air Base, and were last reported as being 'non-operational' in July 2007.

As mentioned earlier, Switzerland had expressed an interest in the A-7, as had Malaysia and Pakistan. The latter, a potentially lucrative deal, was embargoed by President Jimmy Carter in 1977. On the home front, the USMC chose the A-4M Skyhawk over the Corsair II. Years later the A-7 was looked at again by the USMC but the AV-8 Harrier was selected instead.

The US Navy Corsair II in Action

Vietnam (1967–73)

On 4 November 1967, the A-7As of VA-147 'Argonauts' began their first combat cruise, embarking on the USS *Ranger*, the first of four tours in Vietnam for the squadron. After arriving at Yankee Station (a point in the Gulf of Tonkin from where the US Navy carriers of Task Force 77 carried out operations) and just four weeks after joining USS

Ranger, VA-147 was flying its first missions, which were to attack communications lines close to Vinh in North Vietnam. Still aboard USS *Ranger*, the squadron then flew support operations in January 1968 during the siege of Khe Sanh. The carrier was then ordered to the Sea of Japan during the USS *Pueblo* incident later that month. Having returned to Yankee Station for further operations, USS *Ranger* was again ordered back to the Sea of Japan following the shooting down of a US Navy EC-121 by the North Koreans on 15 April 1968. In September 1969, VA-147 re-equipped with the A-7E and redeployed to Vietnam on the USS *America* in 1970 and then on the USS *Constellation* during 1971 and 1972.

During the Easter Offensive, the squadron took part in Operation Freedom Train, which involved a large number of tactical sorties on targets in South Vietnam and further targets in the southern reaches of North Vietnam. VA-147 returned to Vietnam for the final time with the A-7A between March and June 1973, operating from the USS *Constellation* in support of Operation End Sweep, which entailed the clearing of mines in North Vietnamese waters.

The first operational A-7Bs were delivered to established VA-215 'Barn Owls' on 1 March 1968 while VA-146 'Blue Diamonds' received their first 'Bs' on 4 June 1968. Both units were destined to join the USS *Enterprise* in January 1969 to be deployed to the Gulf of Tonkin. The carrier suffered a major fire off Hawaii on 14 January 1969 when a Zuni rocket exploded. As a result, *Enterprise* was only on combat duty for thirty-five days, and while the carrier was being repaired, A-7Bs were delivered to VA-25 and VA-86, which joined USS *Ticonderoga* in March 1969.

The mark had a busy war record which included fifteen cruises, resulting in the loss of eleven aircraft in action and a dozen more through accidents. Of the combat losses, seven were as a result of anti-aircraft fire, one was to a SAM and three others were unaccounted for. Over an eight-year period, A-7Bs carried out forty-five cruises; the last of them, in 1977, was aboard the USS *John F. Kennedy*. From then on, the A-7B only served the Navy reserves until it was withdrawn in January 1987.

The A-7Cs of VA-82 and VA-86 'Sidewinders' both deployed to Vietnam aboard the USS *America*. VA-82 was originally established with the A-7A on 1 May 1967 and, after two tours in Vietnam, re-equipped with the A-7E in August 1970. However, thanks to unforeseen problems with the A-7E's TF41 engine, the unit re-equipped again with the A-7C. The unit then returned to Vietnam between June 1972 and March 1973, operating from the USS *America*. One of VA-82's successes during this tour was an attack on the Thank Hoa Bridge which instantly disrupted the main artery of the North Vietnamese supply lines. Up to this point, the bridge had appeared to be immovable but an accurate attack by just four A-7Cs, carrying a pair of 2,000 lb Walleyes and two 2,000 lb Mk 84 bombs between them, managed to take out the central piling, causing the main span to break neatly in half; the bridge never featured in the conflict again.

The A-7E began contributing to air operations over Vietnam from May 1970, beginning with VA-146 and VA-147 on board the USS *America*. The A-7E was a major player in the close-air support role over both North and South Vietnam, its bombing and navigation systems proving to be a major asset. When maintained efficiently, the weapons systems of the A-7 Corsair II proved to be considerably more reliable and accurate than those employed by the A-6 Intruder, A-3 Skywarrior and A-5 Vigilante. The majority of US Navy air wings, which had been operating the A-4 Skyhawk and early versions of the A-7, re-equipped with the A-7E. In 1972, the A-7E played a key role when Haiphong harbour was mined, and an even more significant role during the Linebacker I and II operations, leading up to the signing of the Paris Peace Accord in 1973.

395 A-7As and A-7Bs and 387 A-7Es took part in the Vietnam War, operating with twenty-seven US Navy squadrons. The aircraft carried out 90,230 combat missions, each of them averaging 2¼ hours in duration. 49,200 of the combat missions were flown by early variants, while the remaining 41,030 were carried out solely by the A-7E. Fifty-five A-7s were lost (out of 100 in total) to enemy fire, the bulk of them early variants, as the A-7E had a loss rate 30 per cent lower, thanks primarily to its better weapons systems which allowed the aircraft to make a single pass over the target rather than risking a more dangerous second.

Cdr Gus Kinnear sits in the cockpit of his VA-147 A-7A Corsair before launching from USS *Ranger*. (*Official US Navy photograph via R. L. Ward Collection*)

On 4 November 1967, the A-7As of VA-147 'Argonauts' began their first combat cruise, embarking on the USS *Ranger*, the first of four tours in Vietnam for the squadron. (*Official US Navy photograph via R. L. Ward Collection*)

Above: LTV A-7A-4b-CV Corsair II No. 153220 '301/NE' of VA-147, during its tour of duty in Vietnam with USS *Ranger*. (*Official US Navy photograph via R. L. Ward Collection*)

Below: A-7A Corsair IIs No. 152664 '509/NK' and No. 153144 '507/NK' of VA-97 'Warhawks', which was established with the type on 1 June 1967. (*Official US Navy photograph via R. L. Ward Collection*)

An A-7A Corsair II of VA-27 takes off from the angled deck of the USS *Constellation* during operations from the Gulf of Tonkin in late 1968. The aircraft, No. 154344, was damaged by AAA not long after and was wrecked at Da Nang. (*Official US Navy photograph (CVA-64-17647-12-68 (PH2 Lincoln)) via R. L. Ward Collection*)

VA-27 A-7A Corsair II No. 153143 demonstrates the aircraft's weapons-carrying versatility with six 250 lb bombs, six Mk 82 Snakeye, two AGM-2 Walleye and two Shrike anti-radar missiles. (*Official US Navy photograph via R. L. Ward Collection*)

Above: A-7A Corsair IIs of VA-27 taxi out for a practice bombing mission while operating from NAS Fallon, Nevada. (*LTV (PR.8566) via R. L. Ward Collection*)

Below: VA-215 'Barn Owls' was the first operational unit to receive the A-7B, on 1 March 1968 before beginning a tour of duty in Vietnam with the USS *Enterprise*. (*Official US Navy photograph (USS Enterprise CVA-65 Photo Lab) via R. L. Ward Collection*)

Above: Brand-new A-7B Corsair IIs of VA-146 'Blue Diamonds', which replaced the squadron's A-4C Skyhawks from June 1968. (*Official US Navy photograph via R. L. Ward Collection*)

Below: A fuel-efficient A-7B of VA-25 (USS *Ticonderoga*) refuels a thirsty RF-8G of VFP-63 (USS *Oriskany*). (*Official US Navy Photograph (CVA-14) via R. L. Ward Collection*)

A perfect formation of five A-7E Corsair IIs of VA-25, while preparing to deploy to Vietnam from their base at NAS Lemoore, California. (*Official US Navy (Lt J. D. Bell (VA-25)) via R. L. Ward Collection*)

VA-195 'Dambusters' re-equipped from the A-4 Skyhawk to the A-7E in early 1970 before beginning its first tour of duty in Vietnam with CAW 11 on the USS *Kitty Hawk*. (*Official US Navy photograph via R. L. Ward Collection*)

Above: Commander Gary Mau's VA-12 A-7E Corsair II, No. 156855, on the busy flight deck of USS *Independence* in November 1975. (*R. L. Ward Collection*)

Below: Another VA-12 machine, this time A-7E Corsair II No. 157581, at Yeovilton in September 1977. VA-12's motto, as can be seen on the fin, was the 'Kiss of Death' while the unit nickname was the 'Flying Ubangis'; note 'Ubangis Express' on the port drop tank. (*R. L. Ward Collection*)

A-7E Corsair II No. 159661 of VA-15 'Valions' on the flight line at Greenham Common in 1976. (*R. L. Ward Collection*)

Grenada (1983)

Under the name Operation Urgent Fury, the small Caribbean island of Grenada was invaded by US forces on 25 October 1983. 1,200 troops took part in the initial assault, which faced a determined defence from the Grenadian Army and a number of Cuban military units. The very first combat aircraft over the island were a quartet of A-7Es from VA-15 'Valions' and VA-87 'Golden Warriors', operating from the USS *Independence*. The invasion force soon increased to over 7,000 troops, by which time the defenders were being routed. The latter scenario would have been contributed to by the A-7Es, which flew almost 300 sorties during the operation and dropped forty Mk 82 Snakeye bombs and twenty Mk 20 Rockeye bombs, not to mention a large number of rounds fired by their 20 mm cannon.

Lebanon (1983)

Not long after the events in Grenada, the Corsair II was in action again, this time in the skies of the Lebanon. President Reagan had made the decision to commit US forces in an effort to end the civil war, targeting Hezbollah and the Syrian forces supporting them. The situation continued to deteriorate when 241 US Marines were killed in Beirut on 23 October 1983 by a suicide bomber driving a truck. Reagan immediately responded, stating that he would carry out retaliation attacks on Hezbollah and Syrian targets in the Lebanon, but failed to carry the threat through. However, the tipping point came on 3 December 1983 when a US Navy F-14 Tomcat was attacked by Syrian missiles and an immediate attack was ordered the following day against the missile sites. It was a poorly planned 'knee jerk' response which involved twenty-eight aircraft, including half a dozen A-7Es from VA-15 and VA-87 operating from the USS *Independence*.

The operation, which took place in daylight, was not a success, and the US force was greeted with fierce Syrian anti-aircraft fire, not to mention a number of SA-7 and SA-9 batteries. VA-15 A-7E No. 157468 was hit by an SA-7 near to Casino du Liban off the coast of

Beirut. The pilot steered the crippled aircraft out to sea before ejecting; a prevailing wind blew him back into Beirut harbour, where he was picked up by fisherman before being returned to the USS *Independence*. A second VA-15 A-7E was hit by a SAM but managed to return to the USS *Independence*. A VA-85 A-6E was not so lucky; one of the two-man crew was killed in the subsequent crash.

Libya (1986)

Libya's leader, Muammar Gaddafi, had been baiting the US for many years, but once he declared that there would be a 'line of death' across the Gulf of Sidra, it was a case of enough is enough for President Reagan's administration. The gulf was international waters and Reagan decided to challenge Gaddafi's posturing by despatching the US Navy Mediterranean Fleet to the region under the codename Operation Prairie Fire.

The operation involved three aircraft carriers of the US Sixth Fleet with 225 aircraft between them. Exercises began in March 1986 and the first of several incidents occurred on 24 March when half a dozen SA-5 missiles were launched from Sirte towards a group of F-14 Tomcats. All managed to evade the missiles, but before the day was over further SA5s were launched at patrolling US fighters. It was retaliation time and, on 24 March, a pair of VA-81 'Sunliners' A-7Es acted as decoys, while two more A-7Es from VA-83 'Rampager' (both from USS *Saratoga*), armed with AGM-88A HARM missiles, attacked Sirte (the first use in combat of a HARM). A similar operation was repeated that evening, and the following day further Libyan facilities were targeted, and at least two vessels were also sunk.

The situation continued to deteriorate when a bomb exploded in a Berlin nightclub on 5 April, killing two people, one of whom was an American serviceman. The attack was

A-7E Corsair II No. 157580 '302/AJ' of VA-82, as flown by Commander Tom Mercer, XO, at rest on USS *Nimitz* in Portsmouth, September 1975. (*R. L. Ward Collection*)

proved to have been carried out by the Libyans and, on the night of 14/15 April 1986, Operation El Dorado Canyon was launched. The main wave of the attack was carried out by eighteen F-111s, backed up by four EF-111As operating out of RAF Lakenheath and Upper Heyford. While the F-111 force struck multiple targets, a number of A-6 Intruders, A-7 Corsair IIs and F/A-18 Hornets operating from the USS *America* and *Coral Sea* bombed a military barracks and Benghazi Airport. The A-7E contingent was supplied from VA-46 'Clansmen' and VA-82, in company with A-6Es of VA-55 and VA-34, all supported by EA-6B prowlers of VAQ-135 and VMAQ-2. While Gaddafi was destined to be around for many years to come, he had certainly been given a bloody nose and his involvement in international terrorism was marginally curtailed but not halted.

The Tanker War (1988)

The Persian Gulf was a dangerous place to be during the Iran-Iraq War and, among other nations, the US Navy maintained a presence in an effort to protect shipping – oil tankers in particular – against attacks from both sides. From 1987 onwards, attacks were on the rise and not just against the civilian tankers but also the US Navy, including the Iraqis' 'accidental' attack on the USS *Stark,* which killed thirty-seven sailors. The final straw for the US forces in the area came on 14 April 1988, when the USS *Samuel B. Roberts* was damaged by an Iranian mine. Four days later, the US retaliated with Operation Praying Mantis and, despite the A-7 being in the twilight of its service career, two A-7E squadrons, VA-22 and VA-94, operating from the USS *Enterprise*, took part in strikes on Iranian Navy ships and oil platforms.

A-7E Corsair IIs, operating from the USS *Enterprise*, carried out a number of strikes on Iranian ships and facilities during the 'Tanker War'. (*R. L. Ward Collection*)

Operation Desert Storm (1990)

Operation Desert Shield was launched following the Iraqi invasion of Kuwait on 2 August 1990 and within a short period of time, over 600,000 coalition troops were located in Saudi Arabia and six aircraft carrier battle groups were in a state of readiness in the Persian Gulf. Despite multiple warnings to leave Kuwait, the Iraqis remained defiantly in place and, as a result, Operation Desert Storm commenced on 17 January 1991.

Out of a colossal force of US Navy aircraft, just two A-7E squadrons were still operational, namely VA-46 and VA-72 'Blue Hawks' on the USS *John F. Kennedy*. Despite their small number, sixteen A-7Es took off before dawn on 17 January 1991, armed with AGM-88 HARM missiles, which struck multiple radar sites in Baghdad. The following day, A-7Es delivered a number of AGM-2 Walleye II missiles and, the next day, launched several AGM-84E SLAMs. The A-7Es performed well during Desert Storm, attacking a wide range of targets from airfields to Republican Guard positions, not to mention alleged Scud missile sites. VA-46 and VA-72 carried out 817 sorties during the Gulf War without loss to the enemy, although one aircraft was written off following a nose gear collapse during take-off. During the whole of Operation Desert Storm, only one A-7E sortie had to be cancelled, giving the Corsair an impressive 99 per cent mission completion rate.

A-7E Corsairs of VA-72 (from USS *John F. Kennedy*) and a single A-6E Intruder from VA-75 take turns to refuel from a USAF KC-135E Stratotanker en route to targets during Operation Desert Storm. (*Official US Navy photograph (DN-SC-91-04959) via R. L. Ward Collection*)

The same formation from a different angle, en route to the target from the USS *John F. Kennedy*. *(Official US Navy photograph (DN-SC-91-03708) via R. L. Ward Collection)*

A VA-72 A-7E Corsair II in action during Operation Desert Storm loaded with half a dozen Mk 20 Rockeye cluster bombs and a pair of AIM-9 Sidewinders. (*Official US Navy Photograph (DN-ST-91-05573) via R. L. Ward Collection*)

Service with the USAF

The 57th Fighter Weapons Wing at Luke AFB, Arizona, and the 354th TFW (Tactical Fighter Wing) at Myrtle Beach AFB, South Carolina, were the first USAF units to receive the A-7D in 1969. The USAF A-7Ds initially only played a minor role in the Vietnam War, flying close-support and search and rescue operations from September 1972, taking over from the A-1E Skyraider. On 29 September 1972, the 354th TFW (made up of the 353rd, 354th, 355th and 356th TFS) despatched seventy-two A-7Ds to RTAF Korat AFB, Thailand, under the codename Operation Constant Guard VI for a 179-day-long TDY. For the following three months, the 354th TFW's A-7Ds carried out, on average, sixty-two missions per day against targets deep into Cambodian, Laotian and North Vietnamese territory. During this brief period alone, the 354th TFW managed 6,568 sorties, accumulating 16,819 combat flying hours.

The A-7D presence at Korat was expanded further when aircraft were drawn from the 354th TFW and re-assigned to the 3rd TFS, 388th TFW. The A-7D was a popular aircraft from a pilot and groundcrew point of view; its general reliability, endurance and its low attrition rate were appreciated by all. With regard to the latter, only seven USAF A-7Ds were lost up to 15 August 1973, when the last air strike was carried out in Cambodia. Of the seven losses, only four were brought down by enemy ground fire or AAA. The first of these was on 2 December 1972, when Captain Anthony Shrine's A-7D, No. 71-0310 of the

355th TFS, was shot down by AAA during a CSAR operation over Laos; Shrine was killed. Major J. J. Gallagher was forced to eject from his A-7D, No. 70-0949 of the 355th TFS, on 17 February 1973, when his aircraft was damaged by AAA, causing the engine to fail; Gallagher was rescued. Small arms fire claimed A-7D No. 71-0305 of the 3rd TFS, 388th TFW, over Cambodia on 3 May 1973, forcing 1st Lt T. L. Dickens to eject; he was also rescued promptly by a USAF HH-53C. The final USAF A-7 combat loss of the Vietnam War came on 25 May 1973 when AAA claimed Captain Jeremiah Costello's A-7D, No. 70-0945 of the 353rd TFS, 354th TFW; unfortunately, Costello was KIA.

The USAF A-7Ds made no mean contribution during the Vietnam War and, by the end, had flown nearly 13,000 combat sorties, made up of 5,796 strike missions, 542 CSAR operations and 230 missions during Operation Linebacker II between 18 and 29 December 1972.

The A-7D continued to serve with the 57th Fighter Weapons Wing at Nellis AFB until 1981, and with the 58th Tactical Fighter Training Wing at Luke AFB from 1969 to 1971. The type also served the 355th Tactical Fighter Wing at Davis-Monthan AFB from 1971 to 1979 and the 23rd Tactical Fighter Wing at England AFB from 1972 to 1981. The ANG began to receive A-7Ds in numbers from the late 1970s and, at its peak in the 1980s, 14 ANG operated the type until it was withdrawn from service in October 1993, making way for the A-10A Thunderbolt II.

A-7D Corsair IIs of the 57th Fighter Weapons Wing (Det. 1) over the Arizona desert; the aircraft are piloted by Major James O'Brien, Captain John Morrissey and Major Guy E. Pulliam. (*USAF (Mjr Ed Skowron, also in an A-7D) via R. L. Ward Collection*)

The photographer of the previous image, Major Ed Skowron, takes a 'selfie' during the same sortie over Arizona. (USAF Mjr Ed Skowron (10,726-71) via *R L Ward Collection*)

A-7D Corsair II No. 69-0205 'LA' of the 333rd TFTS based at Davis-Monthan AFB, Arizona. (USAF (Mjr Ed Skowron (*10,725-71) via R. L. Ward Collection*)

Above: A-7D Corsair II No. 69-0239 'MR' of the 353rd TFS based at Myrtle Beach, South Carolina. (*USAF via R. L. Ward Collection*)

Below: A-7D Corsair IIs of the 353rd TFS prepare to taxi at Cannon AFB, New Mexico, to participate in firepower demonstrations at Fort Sill, Oklahoma. (*USAF/LTV via A. L. Schoeni via R. L. Ward Collection*)

Above: A pair of 354th TFW A-7D Corsair IIs and a 13th TFS, 432nd TRW F-4D Phantom, during an operation in 1972. (*USAF via R. L. Ward Collection*)

Below: A-7D Corsair II No. 72-0180 of the 166th TFS, Ohio ANG, in 1977; the unit would take part in Operation Just Cause in 1989. (*USAF via R. L. Ward Collection*)

In a vibrant red, white and blue colour scheme, this black and white image of A-7D Corsair II No. 70-1048 in its USAF Bi-Centennial markings does not do this 188th TFS, New Mexico ANG, aircraft justice. (*R. L. Ward Collection*)

Worthy of mention are the A-7Ds of the 166th Ohio ANG and the 175th TFS of the South Dakota ANG, who flew close support operations in December 1989 when US forces removed President Manuel Noriega from power under the codename Operation Just Cause.

While not regarded as a combat loss, the terrorist attack carried out by the Puerto Rican group Ejérciti Popular Boricua on 12 January 1981 was the worst peacetime incident ever suffered by the USAF in a 'domestic act'. The 'victims' were eight A-7Ds of the 198th TFS, 15th TFG, Puerto Rico ANG, based at Muniz. The attack cost the US taxpayer $45 million, and following the incident security was, unsurprisingly, bolstered!

US Navy Retirement

Following the conclusion of Operation Desert Storm, the A-7E was quickly withdrawn from US Navy service when VA-46 and VA-72 were disbanded on 30 May 1991. Unusually, the US Navy had already brought their A-7s' careers to an end when VA-204 retired the Corsair II on 1 May 1991 to make way for the F/A-18A and a rebranding to VFA-204. This only left the land-based A-7s of VAQ-33 at NAS Key West, VAQ-34 at NAS Patuxent River and the NSWC at NAS Fallon, which had all been retired by 1 April 1992. The final examples of the A-7 in the US Navy inventory were removed by late 1994 and all remaining aircraft had been disposed of at AMARC, Davis-Monthan AFB, by 1998.

A-7 Corsair Technical Information

A-7 Corsair II Engine

Type	Powerplant
A-7A	10,900 lb Pratt & Whitney TF30-P-6 Turbofan
A-7B	12,200 lb TF30-P-8
A-7C	12,200lb TF30-P-8
	14,500 lb Allison TF41-A-1
A-7D	14,500 lb TF41-A-1
A-7E	14,500 lb TF41-A-1
YA-7F	26,000 lb (Wet) Pratt & Whitney F100-PW-220
TA-7C	12,200 lb TF30-P-8
	TF41-A-402
A-7P	TF30-P-408

A-7 Corsair II Performance (mph, Mach and feet)

Type	Max Speed	Cruise	Climb Rate	Service Ceiling	Range
A-7A	680 mph	580 mph	5,000 ft/pm	49,200 ft	4,100 miles*
A-7B	683 mph	580 mph	7,920 ft/pm	43,900 ft	3,100 miles*
A-7D	663 mph**	507 mph	10,900 ft/pm	38,800 ft	3,000 miles*
A-7E	690 mph***	580 mph	-	49,200 ft	-
YA-7F	Mach 1.2	-	-	55,000 ft	2,302 miles****

* Ferry Range
** At 7,000 ft
*** At Sea Level
**** With 4 x 300-gallon drop tanks

A-7 Corsair II Weights (all pounds)

Type	Empty	Combat	Gross	Maximum
A-7A	15,105	-	31,950	34,500
A-7B	16,100	-	29,800	37,000
A-7D	19,700	-	38,000	42,000
A-7E	19,100	-	-	42,000*
YA-7F	23,068	-	-	46,000*

* Max Take-Off

A-7 Corsair II Dimensions (feet and inches)

Type	Span	Length	Height	Wing Area
A-7A	38 ft 9 in.	46 ft 1½ in.	16 ft 2 in.	375 sq/ft
A-7B	38 ft 9 in.	46 ft 1½ in.	16 ft 2 in.	375 sq/ft
A-7D	38 ft 9 in.	46 ft 1½ in.	16 ft 1 in.	375 sq/ft
A-7E	38 ft 9 in.	46 ft 1½ in.	16 ft ¾ in.	375 sq/ft
YA-7F	38 ft 9 in.	50 ft ½ in.	16 ft 11 in.	-

A-7 Corsair Armament/External Stores

A-7A

2 x Colt-Browning 20 mm Mk 12 cannon with 600 rpg. Up to 15,000 lbs of ordnance on eight hardpoints

A-7B

2 x Colt-Browning 20 mm Mk 12 cannon with 600 rpg. Up to 15,000 lbs of ordnance on eight hardpoints

A-7D

1 x General Electric M61A1 Vulcan rotary cannon with 1,000 rounds. Up to 15,000 lbs of ordnance on eight hardpoints

A-7E

1 x General Electric M61A1 Vulcan rotary cannon with 1,000 rounds. Up to 15,000 lbs of ordnance on eight hardpoints

YA-7F

1 x General Electric M61A1 Vulcan rotary cannon with 1,000 rounds. Up to 17,000 lbs of ordnance

Glossary

AAA	Anti-aircraft fire ('Triple-A')
AB	Air Base
AFB	Air Force Base
AGM	Air to Ground Missile
AMARC	Aerospace Maintenance and Regeneration Center
ANG	Air National Guard
CAW	Carrier Air Wing
BIS	Board of Inspection & Survey
BuAer	Bureau of Aeronautics
DBR	Damaged Beyond Repair
ECM	Electronic Counter-Measures
FAP	Força Aérea Portuguesa
FFAR	Folding-Fin Aircraft Rocket
FIP	Fleet Introduction Programme
FLIR	Forward Looking Infrared
FN	French Navy
FW	Fighter Wing
HARM	High-Speed Anti-Radiation Missile
HOTAS	Hands On Throttle-And-Stick
HUD	Head Up Display
IRBM	Intermediate Range Ballistic Missile
IRST	Infrared Search and Track
KIA	Killed in Action
LTV	Ling-Temco-Vought
MCAS	Marine Corps Air Station
NATC	Naval Air Test Centre
PMTC	Pacific Missile Test Center
rpg	rounds per gun
RTAF	Royal Thai Air Force
RWR	Radar Warning Receiver
SLAM	Supersonic Low Altitude Missile
TDY	Temporary Duty
TFG	Tactical Fighter Group
TFS	Tactical Fighter Squadron
TFTS	Tactical Fighter Training Squadron
TFW	Tactical Fighter Wing
USAF	United States Air Force
USMC	United States Marine Corps
USS	United States Ship
VA	Fixed Wing Attack
VAQ	Fixed Wing Electronic-Attack Squadron
VMAQ	Tactical Electronic Warfare Squadron